Those were the days ... ™
VELOCE

Don Hayter's
MGB Story

– The birth of the MGB in MG's Abingdon Design & Development Office

308L

T0386657

Also from Veloce –

www.veloce.co.uk

First published in September 2012. Reprinted in May 2014 & March 2018 by Veloce Publishing Limited, Veloce House, Parkway Farm Business Park, Middle Farm Way, Poundbury, Dorchester, Dorset, DT1 3AR, England.
Tel 01305 260068/Fax 01305 250479/e-mail info@veloce.co.uk/web www.veloce.co.uk or www.velocebooks.com.
ISBN: 978-1-845844-60-8 UPC: 6-36847-04460-2

Readers with ideas for automotive books, or books on other transport or related hobby subjects, are invited to write to the editorial director of Veloce Publishing at the above address.

British Library Cataloguing in Publication Data – A catalogue record for this book is available from the British Library. Typesetting, design and page make-up all by Veloce Publishing Ltd on Apple Mac. Printed and bound by CPI Group (UK) Ltd, Croydon, CR0 4YY.

Contents

Acknowledgements

I would like to record my thanks to all the MG workers from Abingdon and around the 'family' factory for their willing friendship and help. Also to colleagues from all parts of the Austin-Rover, Leyland and Triumph group, who provided expertise and design ability over many years.

Many of the pictures in this book were provided by BMC, Cowley Photographic Dept and Nuffield Public Relations Office, Longbridge from 1956-1980. Negatives and originals are still held at The British Motor Heritage site at Gaydon. Separate pictures by visiting photographers are identified by author or source involved, where known.

Thanks also to the MG Car Club in Abingdon for pictures and help.

Finally, I thank my wife, Mary, for her support (nagging me to get words on paper), and endless patience while the desk and tables were smothered with MG history.

Foreword

From 'A' to 'B' and beyond

I started writing this book after much encouragement from car enthusiasts who had attended my lectures, arranged by MG Car Club groups in England, USA, Canada, South Africa, Australia, and, most recently, America.

I had retained photographs, slides and records from my time spent working in the design departments of Pressed Steel and MG at Abingdon, and felt that the background – how, why and when – was of interest.

More than a picture book, it would feature my own design-based experience of working at MG over many years, with the intention of providing factual design-related information and crediting the many friends and colleagues I worked with until MG closed in 1980.

My career progressed from Detail Draughtsman to Project Engineer, then finally Chief Design and Development Engineer. I began at MG under Syd Enever in 1956, with Body Designer Jim O'Neill, Chassis Engineer Harry White, and Development Engineer Alec Hounslow. Syd retired in 1970 and Roy Brocklehurst became Chief until 1973, when he moved to Longbridge, and I became responsible for design and engineering.

A personal introduction

I suppose my interest in curves of the mechanical kind began during my apprenticeship at Pressed Steel Company in Oxford in the aircraft drawing office, where I was involved in drawing parts of wings and fuselages: the first curvy thing I drew was a 500lb bomb nose! During the war we worked on various aircraft – the Gloucester F9-40, the Avro Lancaster main planes – plus midget submarines, sea and parachute mines, armoured cars and other bits and pieces.

The car industry restarted in 1946; dies and press tools came out of storage and were degreased and updated with minor modifications. Pressed Steel had made bodies and pressings for Morris, Ford, Hillman, Humber, Jaguar and Rolls-Royce, and gradually new contracts came through for new models and shapes from its designers.

My own involvement was as a junior draughtsman and, as I progressed, detail designer and layout drafting. A new body shape came along with beautiful long sweeping curves – the Jaguar XK120 – which really fired my imagination! It looked great as a drawing, before we even saw the first wooden patterns or the first panel pressings. I worked on creating new body panels for Triumph, Austin, Rolls-Royce, Jaguar and MG – my first contact with the company and its ZA Magnette.

The ZA Magnette was developed to a full-size model, and I recall director Gerry Palmer and Jim O'Neill from Morris Motors (next door) bringing their drawings to work from. We drew and issued full-size detail layout drawings for production pressing. Bert Thickpenny was a colleague on this project, coming from Tickford at Newport Pagnell, and we worked together on the doors, side body shapes, and trunk lid area. Bert later went back to Tickford (then taken over by Aston Martin), and we met again when I moved to the Aston Martin site in West London in 1954.

More design work came in for the new Rover P1, a big Austin saloon, and the Jaguar S-type, although this was only body panel work, not complete cars, and I realised I would have to move on from Pressed Steel to gain more experience.

I saw an advert in a motoring magazine for a job at Aston Martin in Feltham, London. I applied for it and joined the company as it was developing its DB3. One of my first jobs was to design a new front end radiator shape for the DB2/4, which was to become the Mk3. I then produced a complete quarter-scale and full-size new body shape for the DB4 on a new chassis being developed upstairs by Harold Beech (an ex-Rolls-Royce designer), and we actually built the first prototype.

At just about this time, David Brown was planning to move the design department north to Watford or Newport Pagnell. Coincidentally, an advert appeared saying that MG (near my home) wanted somebody. I applied and joined MG in 1956, and that was where everything started.

Don Hayter

Early days & prototypes

I first joined the design office at MG in Abingdon at the beginning of February 1956, following an interview with Syd Enever and Jim O'Neill. Aston Martin had decided to move its design department from Feltham in London up to Newport Pagnell, and the MG post offered something closer to home and more production-orientated, which I felt would benefit me.

I didn't realise when making the move to MG that many of the prewar staff – who really made the company what it was – were still there. This meant I was fortunate enough to meet the likes of racing expert Reg Jackson, who, along with my boss, Syd Enever, coaxed a lot of horsepower out of the engines. In my opinion, Syd was the most underrated person in the car industry at the time. There was also Bert Wirdnam, works manager Ces Cousins – the first employee when Cecil Kimber started the company in Oxford – and, of course, John Thornley, who was an excellent boss, and well-respected throughout the works. These people, and many more, possessed the background knowledge required to make the transition back to car production after wartime, and really got going again, especially with the TC.

John Thornley had gone to America in 1946 to help set up a sales and service organisation for the cars there, and for returning US forces personnel who had bought these little English sports cars while in the UK. The start of the American love affair!

I soon learnt that MG was a very small cog in a very big wheel. When I joined the Nuffield Organization of MG it was already very much tied up with the Leonard Lord/Longbridge side of the business. All the companies that supplied us with bodies, axles, engines and gear boxes had to get approval and support from Leonard Lord/Longbridge. Some of these companies were traditionally used by MG: Dunlop for wheels and tyres, Rubery-Owen for fuel tanks and wheels, Auster Windshields, Weathershields and Wilmot Breeden for door locks. This meant chasing around a large area of the Midlands to get parts designed and a commitment to manufacture; a time-consuming business.

The drawing office at MG, as I joined it, was on a mezzanine floor at the top end of B Block, with stairs at both ends. One set of stairs led to the Development Department run by Alec Hounslow, with Henry Stone as his foreman, whilst the other set led to the Competitions Department directly below us, run by Marcus Chambers, with Dougie Watts as his senior foreman managing the cars. This link between Development and Competitions worked well, but it quickly became clear that Competitions needed more space, and some of the doubling up of work was causing problems, too, thus the department relocated to the other end of B Block. As a result, Development acquired a lot more working space, more lifts to raise cars on, and more storage space for parts and tools.

It should be remembered, of course, that the design of MGs had been based at Cowley for a long time, still under Gerry Palmer – the major Morris directors looking over his shoulder – and it wasn't until 1954 that the MG drawing office became independent. It continued to report to Cowley, but had its own design team under Syd Enever.

The early design for what became the MGA was created by Syd on a T-type chassis (the Gordon Phillips car), but it didn't really take-off until John Thornley and

Syd got the okay from Morris-Cowley directors to build three prototypes, which they entered in the Le Mans 24 Hour race in June 1955.

The design section itself was very small: Reggie Miles and Percy Lay looked after all the records, and Jimmy O'Neill, Harry White, Terry Mitchell, and Dennis Williams made up the design team.

I joined this setup from the outside, responsible for body engineering under Jimmy O'Neill. Roy Brocklehurst had been an apprentice at MG before spending time in the RAF, and returned to work in the chassis section. Roy and I worked closely together right up until he was promoted and took over from Syd, who retired in 1971. Roy, of course, did very well, and was head-hunted by our director, Charlie Griffin. He went on to become Chief Vehicle Engineer at Longbridge.

The first job in the body section I remember doing was quite a small one. I had to draw up, and have fitted, an access panel on the MGA body, under the front left-hand wheelarch, to access the bolts between the exhaust manifold and exhaust pipe on the twin-cam engine installation. I had to visit Oxford Radiators branch, and began making relationships in the organization that I was to develop over the next 26 years.

Cars in production at the time included the ZA Magnette, RME and RMH, Riley Pathfinder, and MGA pushrod 1500. The MGA 1500 was actually about to become 1600, which required minimal changes to achieve. There were two cars under development at MG: one with the Morris Engines' (Eddie Maher) unit under continuous development, and the other with the Appleby-designed Austin twin-cam engine.

A prototype of the MGA, the HMO6, was also being developed. The prototype was a maroon, alloy-bodied version, and it went into production with only minimal changes to the configuration of some of the openings (boot/trunk lid and bonnet). The prototype was later cut-up. This car will have been mentioned in Henry Stone's book *MG Mania*.

The Pathfinder model was running the big four-cylinder, 2-litre power unit, and I became involved by making changes for rationalisation purposes, changes being considered by Cowley, which planned to use a Wolseley six-cylinder version.

There was also a Wayfarer down in the garage that we used as transport. It consisted of a Riley Pathfinder body, still with the right-hand gear change, and 1.5-litre Riley engine from the RME series: a rather under-powered, but nice, quiet motor car. The garage also had a Special Six light-bodied version of the Riley 2.5-litre saloon, which MG Development Department ran for some time. I drove it several times, and remember it had quite heavy self-centering steering. During one drive the car got a puncture that rapidly deflated the tyre just before a corner. The car wanted nothing more than to go absolutely straight on, while I fought to direct it into the corner. The five seconds or so it took to get the car round enough of the corner to stop safely was the hardest work I ever did!

There was another car in development that looked like a standard Pathfinder, but in fact had Dunlop disc brakes all-round, fitted as a trial for production that eventually never happened. The handbrake action was to the rear discs, although, thinking about it, it may well have been additional pressure pads on the disc itself. The handbrake always needed adjusting, and was not reliable, the main reason for that particular system not ever being followed-up.

During this early period of my time at MG, as mentioned, Development was located at the top end of B

Quarter-scale models of original EX 181 and proposed lower Midget-based EX 233.

Quarter-scale Harry Herring models:
GT Coupé by Jim O'Neill (left); GT Coupé
MGA by D H (centre); early MGB lines
– new radiator, inset headlamps and
vestigial tail fins (right).

Block, with Competitions at the other. Marcus Chambers was running the Competitions Department, with Miss Jinks as his secretary.

A special version of the TF arrived from Cowley. It was clearly a prototype, with heavily-modified front wings that still looked like flared wings so that production-made pressings could be formed, and the roof had a steel support panel to help shape it and provide a simpler, flush-folding mechanism to drop down in the rear bay. The radiator and grille were still the same, but the body had lots of mods on it, so that it looked like a TF but wasn't. It was a Gerry Palmer exercise, and I don't know of any photographs to verify its existence.

Towards the end of the MGA's life span we received a car from Frua in Italy that had been commissioned by Longbridge directors. This was a very special bodied, coachbuilt car, which had an alloy body that weighed much more than the MGA's, and was designed to meet the 'flashier' requirements of the American market. The car was well-photographed, and pictures do exist. I was commissioned to take all the body lines from it, and produced a quarter-scale drawing to very accurately represent this particular car. Customs and Excise insisted on an Import Bond for the car, which meant it either had to be cut up, or MG faced a very large tax bill. Paying the tax bill wasn't a feasible option, so it was decided not to proceed with production. Amazing that a car worth all that money was cut to pieces with a flame cutter in front of Mr Fishpool, the Customs and Excise Officer from Abingdon!

Around this time, Development boss Alec Hounslow was tasked with producing, by 'knife and fork methods,' a version of the Magnette. He actually took a hacksaw to a car and, with help from two of the lads, cut off the front end to produce an Austin Westminster-engined 2-litre version with new bonnet and radiator and slightly bigger wheels and tyres. It simply looked like a chunky Magnette from the front, but, being quite a light car for the size of engine, had very high performance. As a result, the car caused one or two unsuspecting drivers to be out-dragged at traffic lights – it used to go very quickly indeed. It ran for some time, but again was an exercise that foundered and no production came from it.

During all this time, an old chap called Harry Herring worked in a corner of the development shop as our model builder. He had served his apprenticeship with one of the original coachbuilders. I think he was with Hoopers at Park Royal in London, and had been through the war and done jobs like making artillery wheels for the carriages and guns, so he was a real hands-on craftsman. He had adapted to working on quarter-scale models in particular, to a very fine degree of accuracy. He used big blocks of jelutong wood glued together to make the armature. Using little templates, Harry made models to within $\frac{1}{64}$ of an inch with such a superb finish that they could be sealed with primer, polished and painted to a standard at least equal to that achieved on a car. The models were also used for wind tunnel assessment, and, when MG closed a large collection, were sent to the museum at Syon Park. One or two models exist elsewhere, but they form a sort of memorial to the work that Harry did.

I don't remember anybody (other than Ernie Game from Aston Martin) who produced wooden models to the degree of detail that Harry did, using absolutely simple, basic woodworking tools. He had no special mechanical aids at all, and certainly no setting-up table. It was all done purely by hand from templates or a wooden base.

He also made full-sized armatures, with big templates every ten inches, on very solid wooden frames for record-breaking models. These armatures very accurately included all the main shapes and apertures, and were sent to companies like Midland Sheet Metal, where alloy panels were beaten over the armatures and stitched together in several parts. The parts were then welded together and dropped onto the chassis, ready for the mechanical items and engines to be installed back at Abingdon. EX219 and EX181, the record-breakers, were created in this way, and components such as the MGB Le Mans front end were made from wooden formers.

The MGC GTS lightweight version was an exception, however. Its big, wooden wing patterns were created at the Bodies Branch Experimental Shop in Coventry by Wilf Silcocks to Eric Carter's drawing lines, although they were finally handmade by the same company, Midland Sheet Metal, at Nuneaton.

During this time, production at MG Abingdon occurred in three areas: the ZA Magnette was in production alongside the MGA line and parallel to the Riley Pathfinder, which was in the process of running down (the Pathfinder model had been introduced after production of the older RME and RMH series ceased).

The parts store was right next to the track in A Block. All the bodies and parts came in on transporters through the bottom of the block, and went upstairs into the body line where all the minor details were added.

Once the bodies came off the transport lorries from Bodies Branch or Pressed Steel, they were mounted on running frames (called stillages) on a guided track on the top deck. On this sub-assembly line, seats were removed, to be refitted later, as were bonnet panels, numbered to be re-matched to the car after engine and exhaust installation. Heaters, wiring and lamps were fitted, and each body acquired a build sheet and number for production identification and records.

Electrical hoists lowered the bodies from this top floor onto an elevated build track that provided access to the underside of the cars so that engine, exhaust, axle and springs could be installed. From here, once wheels and tyres were fitted, each car descended onto the guided track again, before standing for the first time on its own wheels. Every car was pushed by hand through the next assembly stages, the slower operatives being encouraged by the cry "Push 'em up." MG never had power-operated lines, and in my opinion this was a major reason for good employee/management relations, which allowed great flexibility and good line communication, the foreman in charge controlling work and assembly line times, and also parts management.

Every car at this time was road tested off the end of the line, completing the usual short circuit out to Marcham village via Marcham Road. A larger circuit was also used when there was something more detailed on a car that needed investigation, or the car required an extended test.

Drivers from the garage and transport side of the company delivered cars to Abingdon station to be loaded on transporter rail trucks and taken by train to the docks, either in Liverpool, Bristol or Southampton. Quite a few drivers came from transport companies like B J Henry, and cars were actually driven to the docks on trade plates. Several cars a day would depart, depending on when the boats – to America, Canada or Australia – were actually in port and loading.

In the 1970s emission control legislation and the need for batch control gave rise to improvements such as a rolling-road engine test, and less need for road testing.

The Riley part of MG & Riley at Abingdon

By early 1956, Abingdon had only a small representation of Riley offices, and these functioned with one sales link – Mike Cooper – who was based at the MG offices under John Thornley.

One production line in A Block produced the last of the 1.5-litre RME and 2.5-litre RMH Saloons, plus a few 2.5-litre RMH Coupés. At Cowley, over the hill in Oxford, Gerry Palmer's 2.5-litre Pathfinder had been designed for production, alongside the Wolseley 6/90.

The Enever design and development contact with Riley was via various models, including a six-cylinder, overhead camshaft prototype engine in an early Pathfinder body with the typical right-hand gear change. The MG transport garage had been given a 1.5-litre RME-engined Pathfinder body called the Wayfarer, to use for general duties. It also had a prototype 6-light saloon, based on the earlier chassis, brought down when Riley closed in Coventry and moved to Cowley and Abingdon.

There was also a standard black Pathfinder, which was improved by mounting Dunlop disc brakes all round, and a slight increase in horsepower. This was a good 100mph car, but it suffered from an unsatisfactory handbrake system that used the rear discs, and was scrapped.

Once production of the Pathfinder slowed, Cowley directors instructed Syd Enever to produce a prototype Riley 2.6, using the Wolseley 6/90 body and engine then in production at Cowley, and commonise everything possible. A new fascia panel was needed to house Riley instruments and identify the marque differences from Wolseley. I detailed and ordered the new fascia panel to be made in burr walnut by Awson Carriage Company in Baginton, Coventry. The company had previously worked with Riley, when Riley was still based in Coventry.

A Wolseley 6/90 production car was obtained from Cowley, and we drew up new radiator grille and bumper assemblies (front and rear), a new trunk lid motif, headlamp rims and taillamp groups to differentiate the proposed 2.6 Riley from other models. A new side moulding was proposed to enable the then fashionable two-toned colour scheme be applied to order.

Lowering body from the top deck onto Riley 2.5-litre chassis. Shows clearly the guide track concrete blocks, as used on all MG production.

First model: a change of styling from the Wolseley by using a side finisher line (later modified).

The rear window aperture and glass line had been similar to its smaller brothers, the Wolseley 4/44 and MG ZA Magnette series. I had already detailed and made the new larger, wrap-round window for the Magnette ZB Varitone, and a version of this was approved for the 1957 2.6 saloon models.

On the original Pathfinder the rear axle was controlled by a torsion bar and panhard rod setup, due to its unique side-mounted gear change. For the Riley 2.6, this was changed to normal semi-elliptical springs and a centre gear change taken from the Wolseley. I drove the prototype to Bodies Branch Experimental in Coventry, where it was stripped and all the new parts fitted as they became available. The new side moulding rear wing-piece created a special problem, as the stainless steel

section had to be formed in a curve along two planes. I was able to negotiate for this to be manufactured by one of our regular suppliers, Pianoforte Supplies of Northampton: a good example of knowing who could do what and maintaining contacts in the business.

A completed prototype with all the changes was approved by directors and put into production as the original Pathfinder was phased out.

The new 2.6 Riley was sold for the first time with a new, two-tone colour scheme and matching leather trim. This was the last MG production involvement with Riley, except for a short run of Riley 1.5 saloons in 1958. These had been in production at Cowley until more line space was needed and production moved to Abingdon, which had the available capacity.

The MGA

The MGA replaced the older T series, and was the first 'new shape' model produced by MG at Abingdon, owing only the front suspension to the Alec Issigonis/Jack Daniels' Y series MG 1¼ saloon design from Cowley.

Background

The design of the MGA originated from a rebodied TD built to be driven by George Phillips at Le Mans in 1951. The car, known as 5.1.51 EX 172, consisted of a new streamlined body fitted to a TD chassis (TD/C5336). It was capable of 'almost' 120mph, which was a big increase over the old TD, thanks to the new body shape.

The problem with this conversion was that the driver sat too high on top of the chassis, and Syd Enever was already envisaging a wider frame to drop the seats in between the sidemembers and the transmission tunnel.

EX 175 – Streamline Midget 1500cc

A new EX number was allocated for an improved Enever body shape drawn by Jim O'Neill, with many alloy panels and distinctive bulge in the bonnet – essentially, the MGA.

The prototype was shown to BMC management in 1952 as a replacement for the TD. At the same time, Donald Healey convinced Leonard Lord that his Austin Healey 100, using an Austin A90 engine, could be a winner, and arrangements to produce this at Longbridge were made. However, there wasn't room for two competitive cars in BMC. MG and TD sales fell, so an 'internal MG radiator' design was applied to create the TF. Designed primarily for export at 1250cc, capacity was later raised to 1500cc when the XPEG record block engine became available.

Do not forget that MG Design was still at Cowley, and it suffered from divided priorities; Gerald Palmer being responsible for the Wolsely range – 4/44 and ZA Magnette, 6/90 Wolsely and Pathfinder Riley. At Abingdon, management saw the need to produce something new, and John Thornley kept pressure on Longbridge to allow development to proceed on EX 175.

The London Motor Show saw the Austin Healey 100 again, and the new 100mph TR2, plus the result of Gerald Palmer's previous work, the Jowett Jupiter.

The styling changes convinced Leonard Lord that a new MG was needed, and the design office at Abingdon was reopened with Syd Enever as Chief Engineer.

1954 saw the first prototype handmade chassis built by Henry Stone, Doug Watts and Harold Wiggins. These were to run at Le Mans in 1955 with handmade alloy and steel bodies. The cars had wire wheels and drum brakes (later changed to Dunlop knock-on wheels and discs all

Ex-Le Mans car in Dundrod form (lowered headlights) – loaned for Swiss hillclimb.

round), and were built to EX 182 spec. An alternative specification using Girling discs all-round was also tested. However, both disc brake versions suffered from poor handbrake efficiency and adjustment problems, so early production spec comprised drum brakes for cost and reliability reasons.

When I came to MG in Feb 1956, these cars were in development, used for engine and brake tests. The first two experimental twin-cam cars were also just beginning to be evaluated: the Austin-designed Appleby engine, and competing Morris 1588cc unit. The Morris version used the basic EPEG block (allegedly), which swung the decision for production in its favour.

As mentioned, my first job was to design an access through the front inner wheelarch panel for the exhaust manifold to downpipe connection, and Syd sent me to Radiators branch in Woodstock Rd, Oxford to find a suitable louvre press tool to get airflow through at the same time. It was here that I met Barrie Jackson ('Jacko' Jackson's son), who later transferred to MG on the B and V8 programme.

The prototype twin-cam had bulges in the A basic bonnet shape. Syd and Jimmy O'Neill found that by altering the existing curve by about ¾in – a simple tooling exchange – they could use a common panel for both basic 1500cc and twin-cam versions. This led to confusion over part numbers later on!

The EX 175 (HMO 6) was also in development. It was well used as a brake development car, and the extensive use of alloy panels was evident in the dents all over it. Since cost controls allowed for only a few 'registered' cars and trade plates at any one time, to bring on or build a new car or prototype meant an old one had to go. Therefore, this car was cut up and parts from it used on other vehicles. It meant that when

EX 186 Special Le Mans prototype quarter-scale model for wind tunnel testing at Armstrong Whitworth.

a replacement for the A was later considered, and a chassis sent to Frua in Italy by Harriman that was deemed unsuitable (it had to be cut up in front of the Customs and Excise man), £1500 from our budget went down the drain!

A year earlier, another handmade chassis was created under EX 179. It was lightened everywhere possible by Henry and Dougie as a basis for a record-breaker. Similar in shape to EX 135, the car was designed by Terry Mitchell to Syd's specification. Powered by a supercharged version of the 1500cc engine, it achieved 120mph at Utah. Originally built as a LH drive car, it was converted to RH drive in 1956 to allow for a prototype twin-cam engine to be fitted. Ken Miles and Johnny Lockett exceeded 170mph with it on the salt flats.

Another exercise labelled EX 183 was designed by Terry Mitchell with a multi-tubular chassis in an effort to reduce weight, and also the amount of large pressings and consequent welding jigs for the A chassis. The car

EX 186 actual car in development ready for high speed runs on the banking at MIRA, driven by Tom Haig.

Jim O'Neill version of the MGA new coupé body. Later redeveloped as BMC1959 by the author.

was tested for a long time with a Dundrod engine running on Castrol R, but this was found to give no advantage.

A special racing body EX 186 was also designed in 1955, for the twin-cam project on the A, but with trailing arm rear suspension. Only one example was built, and it was tested to 140mph at MIRA by our development driver Tom Haig (racing forbidden by the powers-that-be). Whenever anybody from 'outside' visited, the car was pushed out the back and hidden. Eventually, rather than destroy it, John Thornley (affectionately known as John Willy) sold it to Kel Quale in California, where it still is today!

Early in 1956, although racing was officially 'out,' Marcus Chambers' Competitions Department, in conjunction with our US importers as the entrants, prepared three cars for the Sebring 12-hour, winning the team prize (19th, 20th, 22nd overall).

This was followed by two cars in the Mille Miglia, with Scott Russell and Tom Haig coming 2nd to a Porsche Speedster, and Nancy Mitchell 3rd in the 1500cc limited price class.

Syd and Ted Lund got together and decided on a twin-cam tourer with the latest specification engine, Dunlop knock-on wheels, and disc brakes. It ran well at Le Mans for 19 hours before an infamous accident with a large dog on the Mulsanne straight and eventual retirement.

In early 1960 Syd Enever had another visit from Ted Lund, and I was asked to design a fastback coupé for him, based on the production coupé, but with a lowered roof,

MGA Le Mans car featured the coupé windscreen, a new roof line, and alloy panels, a larger fuel tank, and 1960 tuned twin-cam engine. It won the 2-litre class at 91.2mph. Ted Lund and Colin Escott drove the car home to Lancashire.

Proposed larger trunk compartment on the MGA by Syd Enever. Modified 1/8 scale model, not proceeded with.

Frua coachbuilt body to suit US markets on MGA chassis: too heavy and expensive.

improved aerodynamics and lots of alloy panels. Running at 1762cc with Colin Escott as second driver, it achieved about 135mph and won the 2-litre class at 91.12mph, beating Triumphs, AC Bristols and Porsches that all had larger capacity, 2-litre engines! The great shame was that EX 186 was already there, tested with a top speed of 145mph, and we never had the chance to use it.

Pressure to replace the A was increasing, with sales dropping in the USA. I had been working on a new body and engine spec for a year or so, basically, still using a separate chassis. Syd had the chassis boys investigating trailing arm suspension, independent rears at varying arm inclinations, and the de Dion setup that Terry Mitchell favoured.

In 1958 Roy Brocklehurst looked at putting the Dr Stuart 60 degree V4 engine in an MGA when the engine was only partly developed. However, all these exercises finished when Roy's and my proposal for a monocoque body/chassis design was given the go-ahead by Syd, and the MGB project began.

Within the series of body styles in the evolution from MGA to MGB, another coupé was developed but never built. Listed under EX 214, it used an unchanged MGA chassis, and we built a full-size model in Bodies Branch Experimental. John Thornley and Syd Enever were very happy with the package, but weight calculations showed that with the then available 1622cc engine, it was not a viable proposition. This convinced me that a separate chassis in volume production was no longer feasible, and the MGB project really began.

My personal memories of the A were preparing the coupé for production at Bodies Branch with Eric Carter, and rushing up and down between Abingdon and Coventry nearly every day. Coincidentally, the black A Tourer I was using had the first Judson supercharger, giving superb acceleration and a top speed of over 110mph – great fun! I also had a green twin-cam, briefly with a MG1 number plate, in which to travel to Swindon when the MGB body was production detailed.

For the record

MGA twin-cam – press car.

MGA hardtop with strengthening bars to prevent the
backlight being 'sucked out' at speed.

MGA production line alongside the Magnette.

Record-breakers

In 1956 the development of Syd's fully streamlined new world record car was under way. The full-size plywood armature for the outside panels was made and sent off to the sheet metal factory, and the chassis frame setup and welded. An engine fitted with the large supercharger was provided to be run on the test beds, set up for driving at the altitude of the Utah Salt Flats.

Syd went to Morris Radiators Branch in Oxford to get special cooling radiators to fit in the body profile, and found Avro Shackleton aircraft units that would fit. Dunlop was to provide special tyres with virtually no tread to run at the high speeds involved, and up to 250mph at least.

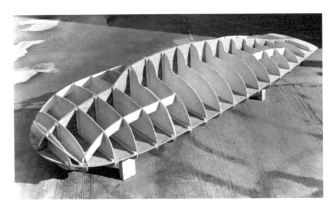

Outline armature for skin panels on EX 181 record attempt car, which had the original long cockpit head fairing.

Tubular chassis frame for EX 181 designed by Terry Mitchell.

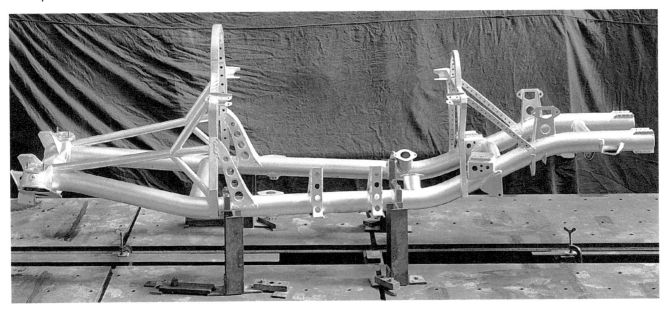

The driver's position right at the front was sheltered by a streamlined Perspex canopy fitted inside the front-hinged body shape, his legs placed astride the steering rack on a very short steering column. Because of the long acceleration and deceleration runs on the flats, only one brake was provided on the rear axle, but a lifting air scoop and intake was fitted on the rear fairing, and activated by the brake pedal.

Stirling Moss had agreed to drive on the attempt, and came down to MG for seat fitting and familiarisation of the controls, and all was approved. When completed and set up, the RAF at Brize Norton cooperated to allow a test run on its long runway. The run was driven by our test driver Tom Haig, who had to 'shoehorn' himself into the seat as he was much taller than Stirling. All went well and the car was packed up and sent to Utah in 1957.

(Left) Stirling Moss in MG Development to approve driving position of EX 181 and assess 'smooth' tyres with Syd Enever (centre) and John Thornley (right).

EX 181

On another subject completely, Brian Moylan rang me on Sept 30th 1998 to ask if I remembered any details of the drive that Jim Cox had in the record-breaker EX 181 on Abingdon aerodrome after we had restored it, and I was able, I hope, to fill him in quite a bit. The original car, which we sent to America in '57 and which Moss drove, had a tail fin on it, specifically requested by George Easton after discussion with Morris Brothers, who did Campbell's car. Bluebird had a high tail, in actual fact, but Syd Enever was of the opinion that a low tail would do no good at all because it wasn't tall enough to provide a stabilizing effect on the car at high speeds.

We fitted one anyway and it did cause a problem, in that the tail fin below the body grounded every time we tried to push the car up the ramp to get it onto a lorry to transport it. That particular part was made removable and the car ran, with the tail fin on, perfectly satisfactorily, with Moss achieving, I think, 245mph.

Subsequently the car was stored for a year with the tail fin removed. The engine was tuned in 1959 to a slightly higher spec, and it was intended to run in two classes – the under 2-litre and over 2-litre – by boring out the engine. It went to Utah again where Phil Hill drove it and achieved the higher speed of 257mph.

The car was subsequently stored in various places: Syd Beer had it for a time; it went into a couple of museums on exhibition, and also to various distributor showrooms. In 1979 I was asked by Peter Frearson, a then director of MG, could I get the car cleaned up and running for demonstration purposes, as it was an anniversary year? I said I was quite happy to do so but that the expense must obviously come out of somebody else's budget. The car went back to Midland Sheet Metal which fettled the aluminium panels beautifully

The car at Utah 1957: Stirling Moss (centre) between George Eyston and Alec Hounslow. Enever in the background.

all over, and it was resprayed with a matching colour to the original green. Then we were asked could we give the car a demonstration? so we approached the RAF at Abingdon, which said yes, we could use the bottom end of the runway. Jim Cox had got the engine running satisfactorily on petrol, although in the original form, it had enormous jets and needles, and ran on MG 2 (a methanol fuel) because of the high supercharge level. It ran at about 32lb psi because of the high altitude at Utah.

Having got the car running we took it up to the aerodrome with cameramen from one of the film

EX 181, again at Utah 1959, driven by Phil Hill increased the record from 245mph to 257mph with six international Class E 1500 to 2000mph records. Phil between George Eyston and Alec Hounslow; Jimmy Cox on the right.

EX 181 restored for a publicity exercise in 1979.

Press launch of EX 181 prior to shipping to Utah in 1957. Left is engine designer Eddie Maher with two unknowns, plus Syd and Alec.

companies; I'm not sure whether or not it was the BBC. The car, remember, had only one disc brake on the rear axle so its stopping capability was not terribly good.

Likewise, sideways visibility from the cockpit was very restricted due to the canopy shape, so we arranged that when the car did the run down the main runway, Les Washbrook and the other people involved in the filming would act as a marker, notifying Jim knew that filming had finished and he could cut off. Jim did a couple of dummy runs at a slower speed, then got up to 50-60mph on the third run. The film people, wanting him to continue, moved the checkpoint Range Rover, which left Jim insufficient braking distance to the end of the runway (a turning circle with big raised glass domes illuminated from beneath). The car had virtually no suspension at all, and Jim was still braking but hadn't succeeded in stopping when he ran out of runway, hit one of these domes, flipped the car partly sideways onto the grass

The car at Abingdon aerodrome after publicity run, during which it was damaged when it rolled.

EX 181 ⅛th scale wind tunnel model, with Phil Hill (centre),
Norman Ewing (right), of the South African MG Car Club,
and the author.

where it rolled, sustaining considerable damage in the meantime.

Thankfully, Jim was okay though very shaken. We had to get the car back to Abingdon to be checked over, and then to Midland Sheet Metal again to get it straightened before it could be put on exhibition. That bit of the publicity was not released and has been kept fairly quiet up until the present day. I gather that Jim has now said he doesn't mind somebody talking about it 'a bit.'

While in South Africa in October 2000, I met up with Phil Hill and he recalled his record attempt. As well as achieving the record, he also remembered a problem: on the first runs, the cockpit filled with fumes from the fuel supply system, to the point that he could hardly breathe, although he stopped the car safely. On checking under the engine access centre panel, it was found that the fuel line had been accidentally partly fractured during the previous refuel and checkover. Once remedied, there was no further problem and the record was attained.

EX 219

In 1959, while preparation of the EX 181 project for the fastest MG record-breaker was occurring, BMC management, in conjunction with Healey, decided on a new Healey record attempt to provide more advertising for the Midget and Sprite markets in America and Canada. Syd Enever was asked to produce a car that would use a supercharged version of the A series engine as employed in both MG-built versions.

The possibility of using a modified EX 179 was rejected because of commitments to its original parts suppliers. I was told to draw up a body shape based on EX 179 to use an MGA chassis and running gear. A full-sized body layout and drawings were quickly done and shipped to Midland Sheet Metal near Coventry, which had made the earlier EX 179 body and was also making EX 181 panels. Engines were provided in durability versions for a 12 hour attempt with a higher performance version for a high-speed sprint. Fuel for running at altitude was provided by Shell, tyres by Dunlop, Castrol lubrication and brakes by production suppliers. A publicity launch day, with a special marquee set up outside MG Development, was held with both EX 219 and EX 181 being released prior to shipment to Utah Salt Flats in America. Tommy Wisdom, the very experienced Healey driver, attended, and was photographed with Syd and Alec Hounslow, who was to be in charge of the mechanics and programme for the attempts. EX 219

succeeded and took records at 145.56mph for the shortest distance, and 138.86mph for 2000 kilometres in class G.

This was the last record attempt by either Healeys or MGs with the A series 1300cc engine.

1800 Morris 7 days & nights – Monza

In 1976 BMC was aware that Ford was going to use Monza for several distance and time saloon car records in the 2- and 3-litre classes. An assessment by Bill Price of the 1800's potential to achieve the existing and projected new speeds, plus its ability to use the steep Monza bankings, was made and pronounced okay. A Morris 1800 was built with all the outside panels in light alloy – no unnecessary sound deadening or trim – and equipped with stowage for all spares on the rear seat. It was in 'Alpine' rally suspension setup, and had a large, 20 gallon tank and alloy minilite wheels – plus a full-width bonnet bug deflector and two-way radio. The engine was tuned to stage 6 with large valves specified, and twin 2in SU carbs with trumpet intakes.

The car and its spares were to be driven across France in a transporter, and an 1800 with competition-standard engine went separately with the SU carburettor expert and timing staff. Competitions had got a timing light system organised to coordinate and confirm results alongside the FIA staff, who would secure approval for the attempt.

We drove to Italy via the Col De Mont Cenis, the transporter's long rear body overhang only just negotiating the hairpin corners on the steep pass. At the circuit, the timing lights were found to be faulty. Repaired by a local expert, all was ready with the pit counters set up and two-way communication working.

The record car was checked, and did some laps

to assess track conditions, lap speed timing, and driver familiarisation. Drivers were Rano Altonen, Tony Ambrose, Alec Poole, Roger Enever, Clive Baker, and Julian Vernaeve, each scheduled to do three-hour stints.

Initial sustained high speed running revealed an exhaust 'stammer' or irregular pulse: audible but not, according to drivers, affecting performance.

Don Law, the SU carburettor expert, was not satisfied, and, after a couple of steady runs when the car was checked for tyre wear, engine leaks, nut tightness, etc, we noticed that the heater area opposite the carburettor trumpets on the transverse engine was sprayed fuel-pink. Don and I realised that this could be due to an intake pulse occurring at between 4000 and 5500rpm, so we removed the trumpets for the next run: no stammer – problem solved.

Tommy Wellman was in charge of the mechanics, and organised shifts for the seven days and nights, as well as transport between the 'Tre Re' (Three Kings) hotel and the circuit. Underneath the mechanics' tools and spare tyres in the transporter with the record attempt car were two aluminium barrels of beer – for medicinal purposes! We were allocated a local contact/circuit mechanic who, every day, cycled the track, checking that all was clear while the attempt was on. In the evenings he rode around and lit small oil lamps as markers on the inside of the track, returning then for a 'British beer.' Next morning an unlabelled bottle of local red wine would appear in exchange.

Late one afternoon Rano reported a striped 'snake' on the banking which he nudged with a tyre and assumed was dead. I walked round there and found a long, deflated balloon from a fete or somesuch nearby, which we later put on his seat. We also saw, to the annoyance of Agip, Italy's major petrol supplier, that

EX 219 Healey Sprite streamlined car built by MG for 24-hour speed record attempt at Utah Salt Flats in September 1959, with driver Tommy Wisdom (left) and Alec Hounslow.

during the preceeding Ford attempt, the company's dragon/bull logo displayed on the grandstand – which normally had flames coming out of its mouth – now had flames coming from the other end!

The drivers did three-hour shifts and we refuelled, checked oil and tyres – changed every 3000-4000 miles – so it became pretty routine. The drivers initiated a competition to see who could do the most consecutive laps to within a tenth of a second, and Alec Poole got 6 and 10 with only one tenth out.

On the last evening of the attempt, with Rano in the driving seat and only John Evans and I on watch, a misfire became audible, and Rano came on radio link to Les Needham, our timekeeper, reporting a drop in power. We called him in on the next lap, and a quick check revealed that compression had gone on a number 3 cylinder (I think). We removed a very hot set of manifolds, water hoses, etc, and took the cylinder head off, to find that half a valve head had disappeared with no visible damage. As we had the FIA scrutineers and timekeepers watching, we had to use only tools and spares carried on the car, so we rapidly found a valve, seated it with a quick tap of the hammer, and began reassembly.

By this time the other nightshift mechanics on the circuit had noticed the lack of engine noise, and rushed to help. In under 20 minutes we were refilling the coolant system and the car was back on the track. We took the record from the Ford Zephyr for 4, 5, 6 and 7 days with 15,000 miles (20-25,000km) at 93.38 mph.

There was considerable celebration at the hotel, with lots of Chianti, and the staff there joining in after the meal, followed by the long drive back, and just bagging the last space on the ferry home.

The relationship between EX 181 & MGB body shapes

When I came to MG Design in 1956, the basic aerofoil design for EX 181 had been drawn, and an eighth-scale wind tunnel model made. This was followed by more detail work and a quarter-scale model in wood which was painted and highly polished.

In parallel with this a new coupé body shape was developed for a new body on the MGA chassis. Being developed in the same body drawing office, direct comparisons were possible, and Syd Enever wanted to use the best aerodynamic shape for the new car. Therefore, the same body curves and sweeps (large radius curves) were available and used.

When the full-size EX 181 was drawn, the MGA replacement became EX 205. The addition of headlamps, taillamps, door, engine cooling and trunk apertures meant the clean aerofoil shape had to be tailored into more practical surfaces road car styling shapes. This, however, made the coupé very full and curvy; too big.

When I took on the design of a more flowing shape, and initiated the change to mono-construction, I did several quarter-scale models until the MGB evolved – though still using the same basic curves, including the similar transverse curves, wherever I could. The record-breaker had to be very long to achieve good penetration, smooth airflow, and minimal tail drag. The developed car cannot have all these advantages and is a compromise, although still with a drag factor bettered only by cars such as Lotus and equal to that of Ferrari! (See illustration, page 36.)

Morris 1800 record car on Monza banking at 95mph.
(Courtesy Peter Browning)

Wind tunnel model, ⅛ scale of EX 181.

Out to play – rally stories

Because of the close relationship we enjoyed with Competitions, Terry Mitchell, Roy Brocklehurst and I put our names down as possible mechanics on any trips needing more staff. As a result, we all did trips to the Liège-Rome-Liège, Alpine rallies and Le Mans. I also went to Monza for a record attempt.

In 1963 I was due to attend the Liège rally to southern Yugoslavia, and was allocated to drive a big Austin 110 (Westminster) with Gerald Wiffen, carrying support spares, and to provide food and drinks where necessary. However, at this time Europe had been very badly shaken by a big earthquake, the epicentre of which was at Skopje in southern Yugoslavia, which nearly destroyed the city. Supplies of medical equipment, food, tents and tools were being sent from England, and one big distribution centre was Abingdon Air Force Base where the big Beverley transport aircraft were sited.

At exactly the same time preparations were ongoing for the Liège rally, supported by all the European car manufacturers. After much discussion it was decided to carry on with the rally as planned, but to not go through the town of Skopje.

MG Competitions was entering Big Healeys and a single MG 1100 saloon, as well as providing support for private entries from the Austin Morris Group. I was allocated to drive to Ljubljana. Stuart Turner held a briefing session, where we were given a detailed programme of stops and contact points with telephone numbers.

With loaded cars going to various key points on the route there and back, we took the Dover ferry and, in our case, went straight across Belgium and on to the German autobahn, through Austria and via the Wurzen Pass into Yugoslavia to overnight in Ljubljana, where the tourist office found us somewhere to stay.

Four floors up in a block of flats, we got a bare room with two beds, a table and chairs. The door opened onto a long, wide corridor, where wash basins and one bath and a toilet at the end did not even have a curtain to afford some privacy. These facilities were shared by the whole floor.

During the night there were several minor earth tremors that shook the building: being four floors up was quite interesting! Breakfast was in a nearby café, and consisted of brod (solid Yugoslav bread), yellow 'something' soup and (I think) coffee.

Leaving (I think) we took the road south to Zagreb and on to Skopje. However, something had upset Gerald's tummy, and an urgent stop was needed en route, where he slipped between roadside trees and disappeared into a shoulder-high field of maize. While doing the necessary he was startled to find he was being watched by several small boys, obviously waiting to beg for money. He beat a hasty retreat back to the car and we rapidly moved off.

Passing Zagreb we continued along the Skopje road, which was to have been our first checkpoint. Nearing Skopje, our route took us along the side of a mountain with a steep slope on one side of the road. Arriving at a traffic hold-up, we discovered that the road had cracked due to a fairly severe landslip, and the repair road grader vehicles were doing their best to repair the damage so that traffic could get through.

On the ring road around Skopje we saw devastation everywhere: a large block of flats split right down the middle, and long queues at the petrol station where the electric pumps had failed. We had to manually operate the fuel pumps, in the process helping to fill ambulances on their way to hospital. Overhead we saw a Beverley transporter aircraft from Abingdon aerodrome, flying in the first of the Red Cross and aid parcels on their way to the earthquake victims. Until then we had had no idea of the severity of the 'quake. The main, normally partly unsurfaced road – with groups of survivors camped alongside it – was in 'washboard condition,' making driving slow and uncomfortable for many miles.

The Peć, Yugoslavia (now Serbia) site ready to service 1963 Liège-Rome-Liège Rally. On a hill slope at the rear was a German controlling gun placement.

We drove on, turning north to Prizren: 'bandit country,' we were told, having to ford a couple of rivers where bridges were damaged or blocked. One of them had a lorry on it that had tried to cross, and was now at an angle of 45 degrees. We came across queues waiting to cross; some lorries were managing to cross where locals were filling in the river bed with rocks and stones. We helped where we could and got across the shallower bits ourselves, then joined in pushing the local school bus across the river.

We arrived at Prizren marketplace and, not liking to leave the car unattended, Gerald stayed with it whilst I went to the bar to get drinks. Populated by beardy, whiskery types, all conversation ceased as I approached the counter. Noticing that the nearest drinker looked faintly human – and that his glass was empty – I pointed at it and asked "Beer or raki?" His big smile and query of "English?" elicited lots of chatter down the bar when I confirmed that I was. They all then pushed forward their glasses and I paid for drinks all-round. It must have cost me half a crown in old money, and was a good investment. When the local shepherds have curly knives stuck in their belts you don't argue. I collected some pies and drinks and we headed out of town.

We arrived at Peć, our first major service stop. We booked into the only hotel and set up the car nearby, with tools ready and sandwiches, fruit and drinks (only squash!) for the drivers. Next to us were Rootes, Reliant, Citroën and Mercedes, and we were busy as the cars came through. No problems with our cars: petrol, oil, and tyre checks only. A Reliant Sabre stopped with the front bumper damaged and fog lights hanging off. The driver, TV commentator Raymond Baxter, yelled "Anyone got a big spanner?" so I piled in with my kit and reattached the bumper to the chassis, and off he went.

Having tidied up we went back to the hotel for a meal, ringing through to Split that we had not seen the MG 1100, to be told it was stopped by the road, but there was nothing we could do.

Later, a telephone message advised us that a red British sports car had been involved in an accident some miles north on the mountain road. We drove out about 20 miles and found the Big Healey on the sloping outside edge of the road, with damaged front wing, wheel and radiator. The accident area was steep mountainside, complete with a deep drainage gully in which a wood lorry was jammed. The outside edge of the partially-surfaced road was a low, rough bank, that fell away very steeply down through brush cover to a stream. Driver Timo Mäkinen had a lump the size of a pigeon's egg above his right eye where he had hit the windscreen frame, and was still dazed, though able to tell us what had happened. Co-driver Geoff Mabbs, who had been asleep, was bruised and shaken but alright.

It was very dark there, the only lights those of the cars and the police spotlights as the very drunk driver of the wood lorry who had caused the accident was being interviewed.

Gerald attached a solid tubular tow bar to the Healey and dragged it onto a level bit of road, away from the 50ft drop through small trees to the river below, and jacked up the damaged corner of the car. By beating

back the front wing panel with the very bent front wheel removed, we managed to nearly realign the steering arm. With a new wheel, the car was just towable, and with Timo steering we were able to get back to Peć. Gerald had said to Timo: "You bent it, you drive it!"

During our repair work the police informed us of another big white car that had broken down, so I went to find it to see if I could help. It was Renée Cotton in a big Citroën with completely failed electrics, and very little battery power or tools. I couldn't help him, but promised to relay messages to the hotel and Citroën service.

We booked in Timo and Geoff, loaned them some clothes, had a shower – in my case brown mud from road dust running for minutes into the drain. The hotel could not help in finding clothes for our drivers, but luckily, being about the right size, I had a spare pair of trousers and a shirt for Timo. These, as far as I know, went off to Finland and I was thanked later. Despite being very late we got them a meal and were invited to join a local party at the bar. Timo, despite his bruised forehead, was in good form, and was soon tucking dinar notes down the bras of the performing belly dancer and local dancers on the floor. The party went on until about 3am: obviously, he had made a good recovery!

Next morning, after phoning base, we towed the Healey to the railway station and negotiated a ticket from Peć to Ostend on an open flat truck. The local police insisted that a soldier guard complete with rifle was to sit with the car until it left Yugoslav territory at the Italian border.

We departed, fingers crossed. Our drive back through the mountains to Skopje and Belgrade airport was arranged, with Timo and Geoff and their luggage already on board for their flight to Belgium, so the barge (A110 Austin) was well loaded.

As if this was not enough, en route following the railway and river, close to the Albanian border we found the MG 1100 in the final stages of repair with a broken front suspension ball joint. Local garage mechanics had succeeded, despite the obvious language difficulty, in getting a new one made by hand at a local garage as arranged by the drivers, Pauline Mayman and Val Domleo. Due to the severe hammering the springs had experienced on the broken road surface, our barge was now also undriveable, with the locating front eye of the left-hand rear spring broken off.

Once again, by the side of the road, we jacked up the barge and completely removed the spring, with additional help and suitable comment from Timo. Gerald knew there was no chance of a replacement, so we undid the axle U bolts, and redrilled and filed out the centre spring location pin hole, thus enabling us to turn the rear spring eye to the front. As the now rear of the spring had no eye, we sawed off a piece of timber we had in our tool kit (for use as an additional jack), and wired it to the chassis with the spring, suitably greased, sliding on it, and taking the car's load.

While we were repairing the spring a lorry pulled up and the local driver – whose fractured English was very much better than our Yugoslav – offered to help. Finding we were English, he commented: "You are in Macedonia and we MUST help you." He was surprised that our combined tool kits were so good, particularly as I had some nearly new small adjustable jackdaw spanners. When we were finished I gave him one as a thank you and promised to send him a postcard on return. I hope he got it!

The repair worked well enough at lower speeds, so with Pauline and Val following us in the 'repaired' MG 1100, we headed for Belgrade airport to deliver Timo and Geoff.

Taking three-hour stints to share the driving the rest of us headed for southern Germany, found a hotel and collapsed.

Next day was routine autobahn with the barge doing 60-70mph on its greased wooden block, which survived to Liège and on to England. I drove the 1100 for several hours on the autobahn to give the girls a rest in the back of the barge.

Gerald and I attended the Liège dinner and prize giving, but I only remember eating and going to sleep, hearing the applause in the distance. Not that it mattered as we got no major prizes.

It was an easy drive next day back to Calais for the Dover ferry and home.

In 1964 I was again offered a place by Stuart in the team for the Liège Marathon de La Route, to go with Den Green to Perast, the furthest checkpoint in southern Yugoslavia. (I still have the original team instructions.) We found we were to be accompanied as far as Novi, in Yugoslavia, by Mike Poole.

Again, using the big Austin A110 fitted with a Healey engine and overdrive gearbox, we set up at the rally checkpoint, with cars due at about three am, and filled up with petrol. There was the usual pressure as the cars came through with no problems until the David Hiam/ Julian Vernaeve MGB arrived with side damage on the right-hand front door and rear wing. The rear door edge was badly buckled in the lock area, and would not close properly. Hiam and Vernaeve proposed retiring as they were having to hold shut the door. Den Green said: "Not on my patch, you don't," and promptly drilled a hole from door flange to wing and drive-screwed the door shut, saying: "Get on with it, the car's running fine, just use the other door." Off they went off from Novi, still grumbling.

Novi, 1964, service point. We left Mick Poole, complete with spares and tools, to do the servicing and collected him on the way back from Perast and Kotor.

Yugoslavia, 1964, Perast service site, and an Austin Westminster with trailer and petrol jellybag, and Den Green.

We left Mike Poole there with emergency repair kit and tools, and drove south toward Perast. While en route we stopped in the evening to find an hotel, and were offered a chalet on the edge of a maize field with meals from the busy hotel – very simple but clean, so we stayed. During the night several tremors occurred, and when we tried to leave the chalet early the next morning, we found the door jammed. Whilst trying to dislodge it the cheap alloy key broke off in the lock! With absolutely nobody about at dawn, and barred windows, luckily, I had my tool kit with me, and was able to unpin and remove the lower wooden centre panel of the door. Passing our luggage through, followed by ourselves, I refitted the panel so that it looked okay, leaving the broken key in the lock. We paid the bill at the hotel, saying nothing, and quietly left, creeping across the path in the maize field to the car. I often wonder what the hotel thought about our Houdini-like exit from the room!

We drove all day, avoiding the longer part of the rally route through the mountains, and that night we took an old wood-burning steamer flat-top ferry down the lake to Perast. We set up at the rally checkpoint by the lake, with Mercedes one side and Rootes the other, again at about 2.30am. On schedule we became aware of the echoing sound of big six-cylinder exhausts coming through the pass. We refuelled the Rano Altonen big Healey first, followed by the other cars, and provided Stayfresh bread sandwiches with fruit and drinks.

On this rally we had towed a small trailer carrying a 50 gallon flexible petrol container known as a jellybag, fitted with a hand pump and delivery pipe nozzle, as petrol was not available on the rally route. Other competing crews took jerrycans which were heavy and took up lots of room. However, Italian team support for Alfa, Fiat and Lancia came in the form of a small petrol tanker, apparently driven all the way by one, obviously very experienced man. After the rally had gone through he opened a side compartment which was already prepared for food, coffee-making and chianti. We never found out how he heated the coffee-maker so close to all that petrol!

Austin A110 ready for service at Perast. In the background are Rootes Hillman cars with Marcus Chambers.

Then it was our turn for sardine sandwiches and scotch for breakfast. A delicious smell drifted past and next to us Marcus Chambers, our old Competitions boss, was in the Rootes camp frying bacon rashers, absolute luxury.

As dawn broke and we waited for full daylight, a local lady with very small twin boys came down to the lake and dunked them in the water, one in each hand, clothes and all, for a morning bath. The boys watched as we got ready to move off, and I offered them a Rowntrees fruit pastille but they seemed to have no idea what they were. So I demonstrated: "Suck like this, see?" They tried and, with big smiles and gestures, asked: "Can mummy try?" Friendliness works in any language, with smiles all round.

Having fueled all the cars and our barge tank, I emptied what petrol remained in the jellybag into a large oil drum, and left it by the lake, sure that someone would find a use for it. As we drove away, I saw a local resident, lighted cigarette drooping from his lips, peering into the drum. No big bang, so he was lucky!

Our next job was to go into Kotor where a Healey recce car had been left for repair following an accident involving Tony Ambrose: we had to pay for the repair work and then drive the car back. I was reminded while reminiscing with Den Green at Silverstone about problems trying to recover the car. The repair garage owner was in contact with the taxi driver involved in the accident, who was using the police to try and get money from the Healey's owners to compensate for alleged lost fares.

Den was taken and held at the police station, even though he could not be charged as he was not the driver. He refused to pay, saying he would contact the taxi driver and company involved, with the car remaining as security, on which basis he was allowed to go. The car was not ready, and more money was requested, so we left it there and headed north toward Split to meet the other service teams.

We arrived at the Hotel Park late in the day to find only a receptionist on duty, and no other staff. It was a public holiday so the kitchen was virtually closed, but he promised to find us some food later. While waiting, I walked to the harbour wall, where I sat and watched an artist painting, on a charcoal outline, the peristyle tower and town buildings. I admired the nearly finished opus and asked how much it would be to buy, whereupon he offered it to me, signed and dated, for the equivalent of a fiver. It is still testament to a nice memory.

Not so nice was the food offered from the hotel kitchen: not very good bacon rashers, several boiled eggs and dry bread. Even worse, at least half the eggs were jet black inside and inedible. Beer and local wine improved things a little.

From there we drove back to Novi and collected Mike Poole and then continued on through Italy and Germany. We came over the Alps at night via the Grossglockner with Mike driving. The car was still heavy and had the unbraked trailer behind. A combination of Mike's keenness and inexperience, and not using a low enough gear for engine braking resulted in brake fade, which was a wee bit hairy until we levelled out toward the bottom of the pass. We drove on to Liège where celebrations were going on, as Rano and Tony Ambrose had won the Marathon. We all joined in the celebration dinner and went to bed happy after nearly 1000 miles in 24 hours.

In 1967 I was invited to be a working mechanic for the Morris 1800 during a seven day and seven night record attempt at Monza. (See Record-breakers).

Evolution or revolution?

Development of the MGB

I have repeatedly been asked: "Where did the final shapes of the MGB body come from?"

The initial design package coordinating chassis and body components, suspension travel, road height, driver and passenger location is stage one. Engine and pedal controls, gearlever location, seating and luggage provision are decided, always taking into account previous MG models for reference, and new car designs for comparison. An overall body outline is then developed, and several possible styles tried in quarter-scale until I had satisfied Syd's requests (to use as many curves and shape developments as possible from the record car EX 181; the so-called Roaring Raindrop). The simple side profile comparison (below) shows where I started. The design office had sets of radius sweeps, and I had my

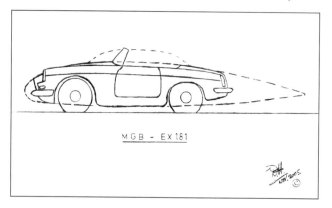

M G B - EX 181

The relationship between EX 181 and MGB profile and curves.

own curves from my time in aircraft production design at Cowley Pressed Steel body office during the war.

At the front end a new radiator shape was centred on an MG badge and large cooling area with 8in diameter headlamps cut into an overall curved profile, giving inset pockets. The front wing crown line was run through to sloping taillamps – newly developed in conjunction with Lucas – giving a nice doortop waist line with small tail fins.

The side body shapes were developed from the coupé design full-size, made earlier but with a distinctive moulding line from headlamp side to rear. The idea, at the time, was that this could be used as the division for a two-tone paint scheme, much in vogue in those days, though subsequently never used in production.

In retrospect, I remember that, over a period of time, when we were looking at how to improve and replace the MGA, the shapes and packages for a completely new car began to evolve. We needed more space inside, more comfort, more luggage capacity: all without the car being too big and heavy, and still retaining a positive MG identity.

Several quarter-scale models were made in tourer form, based on the MGA chassis, finishing up with a coupé (EX 214), which was made as a full-size replica at Bodies Branch and numbered BMC1959. All of these exercises were constrained by the MGA chassis dimensions, and meant a separate body with its own structure, which had to be joined to the chassis. This involved mounting brackets and seals at the joints, plus more final connections and body wiring harness links in the moving production process. It was also heavier in that the body had to be stiff enough in its own right to be handled and shipped for mounting at a different factory.

In those days the chassis pressings were made by

Thompsons in the Midlands, and body assemblies at Bodies Branch in Coventry, with regular lorry transporter runs to Abingdon. It's worth remembering that MG has always been an assembly factory, depending on outside supply from component manufacturers all over the Midlands. Some of these suppliers were within the original Nuffield or Austin groups, and design had to use what parts were available, like engines and associated components, axles and suspensions, and body parts.

Just over the hill in Oxford, the body plant, Pressed Steel, had supplied the Magnette ZA and ZB for several years, and our cooling systems were provided by Radiators Branch in North Oxford.

During 1958 it had become apparent that a new approach to production was needed, and Chief Engineer Syd Enever decided to produce a completely new car using monocoque construction. This would need a stressed floor and sill platform, so Roy Brocklehurst and I drew up a proposed inner and outer composite sill, plus a deep centre-tunnel section. A length of sill section was fabricated, solidly clamped at each end and twisted to assess torsional performance. This was going to depend completely on spot-welding three thicknesses together, so body supplier Pressed Steel was consulted for a first opinion and advice on what became known as safety critical spot-welding. This later assumed some importance because, during the early production days at Swindon, power cuts and voltage reductions actually halted production when full-weld strength could not be guaranteed.

Once the decision was made to proceed, things moved very quickly. I had drawn a new body shape evolved from my previous attempts, and Harry Herring, our model-maker, had made a quarter-scale model in jelutong, a very stable South African wood. Chromium-plated parts such as hub caps and headlamp rims were cast in brass, polished and plated. The wood model was given several coats of primer and painted a metallic green, then finally assembled and viewed for approval by directors. John Thornley and Syd Enever must have done a good sales job on this as we got the okay to go to full-size. I drew up the full-size lines, traced and printed them off, and gave sets to Bodies Branch for the creation of the full-size wooden pattern model, and to Pressed Steel to draft production pressings.

This was the first time we had worked with the new Body Plant at Stratton St Margaret in Swindon. Geoff Robinson was Chief Engineer there, and with him was Bob Doyle, both men former Cowley Body Plant engineers with whom I had worked during my time there. All the design layout men were ex-aircraft designers from Vickers Supermarine who had successfully transferred to the motor industry when their factory closed.

During the time that the details of the inner structure of the body were being drawn and developed, I worked in Coventry at Bodies Branch in Quinton Road, next to the Armstrong-Siddeley car factory. The ex-Nuffield factory was in two parts, separated by a road, across which all the parts and assemblies had to be carried in trucks. At the time, Bodies Branch was making MGA Tourer and Coupé bodies, and the Morris Minor Traveller steel and timber body. The on-site woodmill machined and shaped all of the ash formers and structure necessary for both cars.

Bodies Branch Experimental in Coventry was to make the first full-scale wooden model for the outside panels, thus providing all necessary joint lines to be agreed with pressing production design and tooling engineers. The seating package, including steering column location, controls, pedals, was confirmed at the same time.

Quarter-scale EX 214 MGB Tourer: the first time I saw the final body shape of the 'B' in development. The model was made by Harry Herring in jelutong wood.

The draughtsman at Bodies was Eric Carter, a man of long experience with whom I worked well designing door lock installations, window winders (new in an MG tourer), hinges, drainage systems for production painting process, windscreen framing, hood framing, etc.

When the full-size wooden model was finished and approved, and all of the panel joint lines settled and agreed with Swindon, the first all-steel body was made in Experimental. We were now able to see in bare metal for the first time what the new model looked like, and where all our design work was leading. At that time we were only considering a car in tourer form, but Syd Enever decided to retain an aluminium alloy bonnet panel, because of its size and weight, but not alloy for doors or trunk lid. Pressed Steel was also building its own prototype in the experimental department at Cowley.

While all this development had been going on, MG Chassis Design had been working on a new rear suspension for the car, departing from the old leaf springs in order to achieve a more controllable rear suspension system with longer travel. Syd Enever had experimented with a fully independent suspension system on an MGA chassis, but the problem was that no differential unit of the right size and strength was available within the group. Terry Mitchell had also proposed a De-Dion controlled axle but, again, a special differential centre casing would have been needed, involving new tooling and extra cost.

The final design for the new car designated ADO23 but not yet confirmed as MGB, was a live axle with parallel trailing arms, coil springs, and a Panhard rod location. This package had the spare wheel sloped against the rear bulkhead, and a strap-mounted fuel tank under the lower trunk compartment floor. The effect of this suspension setup was to stress the rear body

and chassis, and the rear chassis members were re-evaluated as a result. The rear cross diaphragm between the wheelarches was made solid and improved. This, together with the previously noted sill sidemember, was proved on prototype test.

While road testing the new suspension on the prototype, both development driver Tom Haig and boss Alec Hounslow were unhappy. Further assessment by Syd and Terry resulted in agreement that all sensed a steering problem from the rear, which was found to be due to the radius of action of the transverse panhard rod controlling the side suspension movement of the chassis relative to the wheels. This, combined with failure of the rod brackets and previous experience, convinced Syd to revert to semi-elliptic springs.

No complete torsion figures for the MGB Tourer were recorded initially, as equipment was not available to us and, in any case, we had no earlier car figures to compare them with. The GT version was later tested in 1976 by Cowley Body Experimental, and confirmed as satisfactory. Also decided were the front bulkhead and pedal positions, which enabled me to establish the seating position, and remember that Wilson McComb, resident *Safety Fast* editor, had said to us: "When you do a new car ensure it is long enough for legs like mine."

So, having, at Syd Enever's insistence, tucked the two six volt batteries each side of the propeller shaft located behind the heel board, we had made room for either enormously long seat travel, compared to the MGA, or two possible locations for the seat runners. Having set the seat as far rearward as possible, we got Wilson to sit in and, surprise, surprise, he could not fully stroke the clutch pedal – one up to Design!

The first front suspension design used similar components to the MGA which, in turn, had come from a well-developed line via the T types and 1¼ saloon. A new pressed front crossmember bolted to the front side members was initially designed to give 7 degrees of castor angle, but was eventually changed to 4 degrees after testing for optimum steering effect.

As soon as we had a fully engineered body prototype we commenced engine and suspension installation.

During the design process for the car we had tried various of the engine sizes currently available or proposed in the group. Chassis design had the 1622cc XPAG engine from the MGA – possibly more highly tuned but not really powerful enough – the heavy, 2-litre Austin power unit, or a brand new development alloy V4 being tested by Dr Stuart. This was to be a 60 degree V-angle engine, for which we received a mock-up unit. Allowing for this and a possible V6 later, I made the bonnet aperture as wide as possible, without incurring the access problems encountered with the MGA Twin-cam.

In the event, none of these units was suitable or available. Fortuitously, Charlie Griffin, our original director at Longbridge, had developed the Austin 1800 with a transverse enlarged version of the XPEG engine of 1795cc capacity. This three main-bearing engine with a new gearbox and non-synchro bottom gear became available and was installed immediately.

During the package development (finalising of the relationship between driver, steering wheel, pedals, and controls), Syd queried the steering column mounting. His long experience with MG and other cars made him insistent that no vibration or shudder should be transmitted into the fascia and windscreen areas of the car. Roy and Terry had made the bulkhead square and securely mounted right out to the sides, but Syd

wanted more and a separate square tube was added between the 'A' posts, or door hinge pillars, which were very strong and linked to the sill sections. The steering column was mounted on the tube and all was fine in testing.

What was not so fine was that, on extensive pave or rough road testing at the MIRA circuit, the panhard bracket on the body at the rear failed. This had been mounted on the curved pressing in the trunk compartment carrying the spare wheel. Even when reinforced it still failed because the new MGB structure – designed to be strong in tourer form – was too heavy.

Syd decided to revert to an improved but still old-fashioned leaf spring design. To get the rear shackle anchorages on the chassis members behind the axle, these were extended slightly. This, in turn, meant that the spare wheel could be laid horizontally, but – and it was a big but – I had to accept the body being lengthened by an inch. All of the body skin lines from rear bulkhead to tail lamps and trunk lid panels had to be re-styled and faired in. Within a week I had completed and re-issued new prints to the Body Plant and Experimental Shop for the production of revised prototypes. At this stage many more detail designers within MG and also outside supply firms became involved in finalising production parts and assemblies. Radiators Branch engineers came up with a design for a pressed fuel tank which had obvious mass production advantages, and was adopted.

Syd Enever, once he had approved the outline scheme, let us get on with the designing, but kept a very close eye on progress. If there was a particular area he wanted done his way, we either worked late to satisfy it or we would come in next morning and find simple sketches on bits of paper, scraps from his sons' (Roger and Mike) homework books, or even on sugar packets!

During this hectic period, when visiting the Development Shop to check on progress first thing, there was always a smell of cooking (or burning). This was Henry Stone getting breakfast after his first fag (cigarette, to you), toasting a cheese roll from the canteen with an acetylene torch. Alec Hounslow, the boss, and Henry entertained us with synchronised coughing after their first fag of the day, both being heavy smokers.

The first MGB with trailing arm/coil spring suspension was never modified, but used for small installation exercises on the body, and finally cut up and scrapped. It had been fitted with the 1622cc MGA engine which was immediately available for preliminary installation and testing. The body had been painted in metallic green and silver to try out a two-tone colour scheme, as these were in favour during the time the MGB shape was evolved. Later, styles and ideas changed and the car was never produced in two colours, although the bright dividing side finisher line was retained until the end. The second prototype with conventional leaf springs and lengthened body was painted black, and had the first full MGB specification 1795cc, three bearing engine.

To go on the new monocoque body I had drawn up an aluminium-framed windscreen with shaped cast pillars, and a wiper system was needed to go with this. Development set up high-speed testing at the MIRA circuit on the banking, and our development engineers mounted a perforated tube across and between the headlamps to provide rain when required. This was fed with water pumped by a hand stirrup pump from a reservoir in the passenger compartment. Testing various blade systems to eliminate wind lift we went quicker and quicker and higher up the banking. At something over 80mph I realised my accompanying Lucas engineer had

ducked below the fascia so he could not see where we were on the banking, but he still kept pumping!

This car also successfully completed the MG specified 500 miles on the Pave, and was used for wheel and tyre, braking, and ride and handling testing. It was retired when pre-production cars, built with production-approved pressings, came on stream, and was bought by John Sharpe, our Senior Development Engineer and raced in club events for a period.

Since MG was small, with lower production volumes than most of the group, tooling money was limited, and we depended on supply companies very much for investment in our parts. This sometimes worked well as they could try new things and processes which, if successful, could be sold to bigger manufacturers. One of these ideas, in which Jim O'Neill, our Chief Body Engineer, was involved, was the use of a one-piece diaphragm seat cushion support instead of individual straps. Jim had previously been in charge of the first development ideas for a new MGA before I came to MG.

Coincidentally, a foam manufacturer and supplier was trying to develop a one-piece, moulded foam cushion in polyurethane to compete with the Dunlop moulded cellular rubber cushion. Getting shape and hardness right to match the suspension ride of the car was a problem. After many long rides over every type of road we could find, we settled on a system which served the MGB well during its 18 years of production.

Two finisher mouldings were developed in a new version of polyethylene black plastic, with a grained finish matching the crackle black fascia paint for the speedometer and rev counter surrounds and speaker panel. This system was, I believe, a first on the MGB, further improved on other cars as plastics evolved.

Safety legislation

I suppose I had assumed that one was always relatively safe in one's 'tin box on wheels' unless something stupid was done or occurred. However, one day, Syd Enever was showing us an Italian steering wheel brought in by a customer. This was superbly made with polished alloy hub, spokes and rim with riveted grained wood hand grip areas. Could we afford to get it made and fitted as special equipment?

Very shortly afterward a very broken steering wheel – it may have been the same one – appeared in the office. The driver had been involved in a serious head-on collision and, in bracing himself for the impact, pushed forward both sides of the rim. The wooden sections had splintered away from the rivets, leaving two sharp spears which severely gashed his chest, although it could have been much worse. The alloy rim was simply not strong enough, resulting in a dangerous failure.

At about the same time the American authorities – in particular, California – came under pressure to deal with air pollution and smog. The car was an obvious contributor to this, along with industry. Exhaust emission controls began to affect engines, carburation and air injection pump installation.

Then the Ralf Nader-inspired 'Unsafe at any Speed' movement began investigating vehicle handling and internal safety equipment changes to the car. Generally, English and European cars handled very well compared with some American cars, which were usually much larger and heavier with bigger engines.

The American government put pressure on the National Highway Transport Safety Administration (NHTSA), which issued a whole series of proposals covering emissions, handling, internal padding for energy absorption, bumper performance, lighting, wiper systems, etc.

At this point all of the European manufacturers, and particularly sports and performance car makers who had a big market in the USA, talked to one another as never before.

The Americans staged a big international show at Dulles airport near Washington called Transpo 72, and the British Leyland Corporation – including MG – became involved in producing feasible proposals to suit our smaller cars; in our case including open two-seaters.

Our director, Charles Griffin, was given the task of showing as many safety systems as possible appropriate to a small car. It was felt that because of possible rollover problems with open cars we would use an MGB GT. I was handed the design installation and co-ordination project with a very tight lead time of June 1972. All our suppliers leapt into action with their own proposals to fit in with MG design ideas. The result was the GT known as SSV1 (Safety Systems Vehicle One), which is still on show at the Heritage Museum at Gaydon.

The issuing by the NHTSA of Federal Motor Vehicle Safety System (FMVSS) No 208, Passive Restraints precipitated intense research, and involved seatbelts which automatically applied themselves to the driver and passengers – very difficult – or installing air bags which were an unknown quantity. We were offered an air bag system by the Eaton Corporation, based in the USA and Italy, as there was nothing yet available in the UK.

After visits by their representative, Peter Giaccobi, we sent an MGB Tourer out to Rivarolo near Turin. Bob Neville, one of our development engineer/mechanics, and I took it there on a four-wheel trailer towed by our 1800 Austin 'landcrab.' We made an overnight stop at

Safety Systems Vehicle, as built for Transpo 1972 at Dulles Airport, near Washington.

Belley, then continued on next morning over the Col du Mont Cenis to the Eaton test base. The air bag system was fitted and wired up in two days, and we returned to MG to set up the vehicle for a test at MIRA.

The air bags were inflated at 3500psi by a compressed nitrogen cylinder activated by a speed deceleration sensor (set above 14mph) on the bulkhead. Similar tests determining air bag size, inflation pressures and the effects of deceleration on the crash dummy heads eventually resulted in a successful system. A film of this development work was made by the BBC's Raymond Baxter and called *Safety in Numbers*.

The Dulles Transpo 1972 Exhibition was supported by almost every European manufacturer, and produced many ideas and systems that met safety standards. Charles Griffin's secretary and I had acquired (as one does!) the job of coordinating the European approach to compliance, and Roy Brocklehurst flew backwards and forwards to Washington with other Leyland engineers to agree methods and feasibility with the legislators. Many of the initial standard proposals were good ideas, but quite impractical in detail, and the effect on big American cars was not the same as that on small sports cars. Continuing changes meant redesign and retesting, even threatening the need to start again at one point.

One of our regular suppliers, Lockheed of Leamington, had been developing two new systems. The first was a anti-lock wheel device that used a serrated wheel on the hub to sense changes in speed, which could adjust pressure almost instantly and avoid wheel locking. The second was a ride levelling system activated by sensing roll on cornering and changes in vehicle attitude. Design changes to the suspension required pressurised units in place of springs, which would keep the car level by increasing pressure on the side affected by roll. An engine-driven pump supplied fluid under pressure to the units on the front suspension and rear axle. This method had been used on ambulances to provide a controlled ride for patients, and on the Ferguson Grand Prix car driven by Jack Fairman. A version of the Rover 2000 was built to evaluate the resulting ride and roll control, and also filmed to show comparison with a standard American Cadillac. Both

SSV1 Lockheed speed-sensing unit on front hub, and front suspension pressure control for wheel movement on roll.

Under-bonnet SSV1 showing front suspension control balance unit at rear left, and speed sensors forward of radiator.

British Leyland alcohol test system with push-button activation for central ignition control, plus airbags and knee padding.

these systems were filmed in action in the MGB GT for the SSV1 presentation.

Charlie Griffin thought that the proposed bumper performance standard, based on the existing USA car industry standard high above ground level, was not good for pedestrians. Coming into contact with high, broad-faced American bumpers would result in severe knee and lower thigh injury, he felt. In addition, the car would then probably knock over the victim and run over the body. A soft-nosed bumper at about 12 inches from the ground would hit a pedestrian on the shin below the knee joint, which would mean less extensive bone damage, and the body would fall forward onto a smooth bonnet or be deflected sideways. Jim O'Neill and I drew up a suitable shape for a foam-filled section which was made up for the GT.

Triumph Engineering at Canley, now the senior part of the group with new Chief Engineer Harry Webster moving to Longbridge, had developed an ignition control system called BLAST (British Leyland Alcohol Simulation Test). A series of random lights had to be correctly copied once the ignition key was turned, with a variable rate of demonstration to make it more difficult. The engine would not start without this.

I recall during the Transpo exhibition being introduced to various bigwigs from the US government on the stand. One very interested lady, the wife of the Secretary of the Treasury, sat in the car and was persuaded to try BLAST. She did so without problem, turning to her husband and saying: "You must have a go!" Before he got in the car we turned up the demonstration rate, and he failed twice before succeeding on his third try. Several Red Arrow pilots – the British Air Display team – were there with the British Ambassador, and tried and passed without a problem.

Another of the proposed new crash performance standards was side intrusion in a vehicle to vehicle impact. Since the door of the MGB, like others, is a hollow flattish tin box a fabricated steel section was added as a stiffener between the front hinges and the door lock area. The door locks themselves already had designed-in anti burst capability. The GT we were using was in bare metal from Pressed Steel at Swindon and sent to Doug Adams' Body Experimental at Longbridge. Tests were carried out to fill the sills, parts of the front wings, rear wing pillar areas and lower doors with polyurethane foam filler to stiffen them.

An MG Tourer was set up quickly in this modified condition - having additionally a connecting interlock peg between door bottom and sill. A crash test was performed between a standard MGB hitting the side of another standard MGB at 15mph. A second test between a standard MGB and the fully side stiffened car was also done. The unmodified car suffered about 4½ inches inward deformation at the middle of the door, the improved car only ½ inch at the same point. Therefore all of these proposals were included in SSV1.

A standard to provide enlarged rear vision in the mirror as proposed would have involved very much

SSV1 with: 1 Panoramic mirror, 2 Windscreen sprayed for head-up speedo readout, 3 Panel apertures to show foam body stiffening set-up, 4 Low, soft, round-nose pedestrian protection bumper, 5 Dunlop run flat tyres.

widened back windows and large mirrors. Not feasible in our GT without major body redesign. Design thoughts on this included an externally roof mounted mirror in a housing focussing down through a hole to a suitable inside mirror. The idea of the standard was to provide the driver a view of all the road, including multi-lane highways in the States. Such a unit was fabricated by the mirror manufacturers and fitted, under protest. We felt that adding a large drag component to the airflow was bad and noisy, and that the driver would be distracted by too much information from behind. This was eventually dropped in favour of better non-distorting or magnifying inside and door mirrors.

Associated with the requirements for angle of forward vision, affecting wind screen pillars and surrounds; rear vision and instrument visibility was to be clear. Smith's Instruments with information from aircraft design proposals, produced a speedometer reading projected onto the inside of the windscreen glass straight ahead of the driver. This required an area of the glass to be sprayed with a transparent reflective finish to show a digital speed readout. This again provided the driver with information continually without having to change his eyeline. All these systems were road tested and installed for a showing of both our MGB GT and a Triumph 2000 to the directors near Longbridge before shipment to Dulles. Our MGB, called SSV1, was set up on a stand at the publicity centre at Hanley together with the Triumph ready for group and Government Department viewing. When approved the cars were crated and sent to the USA Transpo Exhibition site on Dulles Airfield, near Washington.

Bracket guides from the door frame controlled the SSV1's automatically applied seat belts as the door closed.

More minor but still significant changes were being designed and tested over this period. The minimum wiped area of the windscreen caused a change to three wiper blades because of the low wide windscreen glass on our sports cars. This was associated with a defrost test at temperatures down to minus 16-28°C which required uprated heater output and modified ducts for demisting the windscreen glass. For us this we needed access to a cold chamber to bring the cars down to compliance temperatures, spraying the glass with fine droplets and then starting the car, leaving at tickover speed with heater switched on and hopefully clearing the windscreen in so many minutes. Heater suppliers Smiths of Witney were most helpful and ultimately successful. Charlie Griffin, in conjunction with Lockheed of Leamington, our brake suppliers, arranged for a two level brakelight system. The first part was actuated at light braking level, say in traffic but a second much more high intensity light would come on for really severe, crash stop braking. With suitable pressure sensitive switching this was installed together with extra lights.

All of this development required that we should very accurately measure the speed of crashes and use high speed filming to see events in sequence as they happened. Sensors were used to trigger air bag actuations above 14mph (at that time) and a 'g' switch to cut off fuel supply in the case of accidents or roll-over. To record impulses sensed by test dummies, a cable fed out from a drum on the car connected with ultra-violet graph recorders on the test facility to produce deceleration traces. Our MG Development Engineers Mike Hearn, Ron Oliver, John Tanner and Paul Murphy went through a very steep learning curve and produced excellent results. Group cooperation speeded up, with Longbridge and Triumph testing being involved

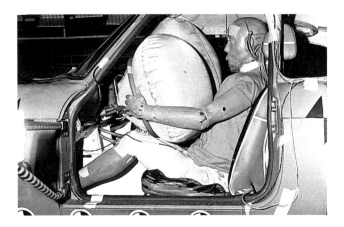

30mph barrier compliance test at MIRA: dummy and airbag in place prior to impact test.

GT roof section stiffening rollover bar for test. Also needed on the Tourer.

all the time. Triumph produced its own safety systems proposals for compliance in a Triumph 2000 saloon of the same period and these came to Transpo at Dulles Airport.

The British Government-controlled activity at TRRL Crowthorne was doing its own crash testing over the same period and we exchanged visits and test information. They were particularly interested in car interior padding in the facia and knee areas which coincided with the USA ideas to some degree. One other area of their research had been into windscreen glasses both toughened and laminated. We at MG had always used laminated and the new increased thickness interlayer to prevent head penetration was welcomed and eventually implemented in all markets. Proof of progress was shown in our barrier testing at MIRA with dummies and airbags and captured on high speed film.

A further piece of proposed safety legislation could, if carried out, have meant the demise of open sports

cars as built at the time. The test proposed an angled ram, pressed at an angle from above and the side, onto cars' roof cantrail and windscreen top corner. This was to simulate a roll over-accident. Since our open cars would be tested with roof down and only having the small windscreen pillar corner, they stood no chance of meeting this standard. One possible way to comply was to somehow stiffen the windscreen pillar and at the same time add a strong roll-over bar just behind and above the driver's and passengers' heads. Several schemes were designed and testing started on the tourers. The smaller volume production GT with changes might have passed, but it was the open cars that the market wanted. Luckily or sensibly, the standard was never issued.

In 1974 an interim standard for a straight forward 5mph barrier test only was complied with by using large extended moulded rubber bumper overriders on the basic chrome bumper cars. The test car was run down a ramp past a timing device to achieve 5mph. To ensure a

Impact-resisting overriders to meet the 1974 ½ model year interim bumper test standard at 5mph.

straight line approach, mechanic Bob Neville volunteered to sit holding the steering wheel straight. For safety he wore his racing helmet, which of course added a little to the weight of his head. Test accomplished successfully he said, "never again!" We had no previous experience of dead stop at that speed plus the rebound effect off the barrier. He suffered a stiff neck for several days and we all learnt something. These model year cars for America

were called 'Sabrina cars' in the factory. This was due to a very well endowed young lady in the Arthur Askey comedians show on BBC television. Americans would recognise the Jayne Mansfield type of build.

The implication of all these changes, which were needed to be able to comply and therefore continue selling cars 'over the pond' was enormous, MG was building about 45,000 cars per year of which nearly

40,000 went to America or Canada and the rest to the UK, Europe and small quantities and sub assemblies (KD) to South Africa and Australia. If we could not comply with the new standards our remaining market of 5000 plus cars was so small that MG might have to close because of insufficient demand. However, we did succeed due to ingenuity and hard work of all our design and development engineers. The specialist supply companies all pitched in with their own ideas, and input, and cut lead times to ensure production would be able to continue with minimum changeover problems.

As if this was not enough, the proposal for the following year meant raising the MGBs ride height in order to meet more severe bumper standards: a change which needed ride and handling evaluation. This involved tyre suppliers together with possible suspension and rollbar changes. The 1974½ model year cars, as we called them, finished up rolling more than we wanted on tight corners but surprisingly with the latest tyres, going through wiggle-waggle test corners as fast as the older cars. Development to control roll was urgent and with stiffer springs and rollbars front and rear we achieved a much more acceptable ride. The benefits of this work were available in the next major alterations to both the MGB and also the Midget which had its own programme.

The 'American' effect on MG production

Once performance standards of any sort become effective, production has to be able to demonstrate how compliance is achieved. Up to this period, when sales to America and Canada had started to grow to big volumes, every MG-built car was road tested on our local circuit west of Abingdon and through Marcham village.

An Emissions Laboratory had been built up in our export compound and here Mike Allison, and a small group of testers, checked and approved production engine and exhaust standards. Every car was now tested on a "rolling road" facility straight off the end of the A Block production lines. A proportion of these cars was then checked again by laboratory and only a lesser number did the road test round the village.

Inspection had a quality and standards operation to ensure parts were consistent and to design specifications, as before, but batch numbers were now accurately recorded in case of query. For the first time vehicle weights became important as the American Standards specified weight groups against emission levels. This became especially important for the Midget as its group companion, the Triumph Spitfire, had an almost identical weight. This meant that from 1975 onwards we at MG had been instructed to use the Triumph 1500cc engine so that a common approach to emission compliance could be achieved. An accurate drive-on car weighbridge was installed next to development for this purpose. It was initially too accurate because we found that, as it was installed in a lean-to structure against a wall, that when easterly or westerly winds blew strongly the airflow over the car altered the weight reading by as much as 10 to 12lb!

All of the original crash testing was at MIRA – 90 miles away in the Midlands – which involved cars and mechanics, plus equipment, travelling there every time. Crash testing was done on basic production cars and on specially modified development versions. We were given permission and a limited budget to build our own facility at Abingdon. A small team of body, chassis and development engineers now became crash facility designers. A 950 ton block of concrete was set into the earth with a 1 inch thick steel plate on its face and a tunnel running right through it at ground level. A carefully levelled concrete track with steel rails approached this block from the plate side, while an engine and cable drive was located on the other. We had to use what was cheap and available in the Austin/Triumph/Jaguar/Leyland group and went shopping. A Jaguar 3.8-litre engine was made available and we found and modified a big axle to drive a drum to wind in the cable. This cable ran through the block and pulled a small trolley, named the ferret, connected to the target car along the tracks with a velocity exceeding 40mph if necessary. The ferret had to pull the car along at just over 30mph but cast-off just before impact, so as not to influence the crash by its own momentum or weight. Too high a speed gave a more severe crash, increasing with the square of the excess, a fraction under was a test failure, so the speed at cast-off point was critical.

Once fully developed we ran many successful crash tests and held a press day to show what MG could do given the right support. Other cars, like the Triumph TR7 and Austin Marina, were also tested at the facility, saving the group quite a lot of money.

The rubber bumper MGB & Midget

American cars had traditionally been built with high bumpers and many were jacked up, in case of a puncture, with monkey-up-a-stick jacks acting on the bumper irons. Our smaller, lighter cars used side or under suspension jacking. The bumper test standard as formally legislated specified the bumper surfaces between 16 and 20 inches above the ground, which was above our chassis heights and so caused an immediate problem. We had to raise the cars at least an inch and produce a bumper surface broad enough to comply. In addition we needed an energy absorbing system that provided a limited damage performance so that no lights or operating vehicle systems were affected by a 5mph barrier or pendulum test.

All of these tests to prove compliance needed test rigs, so we built our own pendulum and a 5mph barrier just outside Development, and set up instrumentation to measure speeds and deceleration forces. Jim O'Neill – Chief Body designer first tried an energy absorbing bumper section in reinforced rubber. This proposed a formed section of conveyor belting riveted onto a steel channel, but manufacturing control proved a problem. He then approached moulding makers and the honeycomb section in polyurethane rubber was developed, riveted onto a steel box section. The problem of obtaining a suitable finish was resolved by chromium plating the moulds. At the same time chassis engineers raised the whole car 1 inch on the suspension, increased the support to the front bumper mounting area, and improved the rear sidemember stiffness. All of this added over 100lb to the car's overall weight. The styling of the final shape was taken out of our hands, being controlled by Longbridge and under Styling Boss Harris Mann the profile was completed. Alongside this, our small drawing office was working flat out on meeting other standards with coinciding dates and effects on the cars.

The 30mph barrier test at that time could only be done at the Motor Industry Research base (MIRA) near Nuneaton – 90 miles away. This used an electric linear motor successfully, but every test completely wrecked a car. Development of a special trolley using multiple steel crumple tubes which could simulate the impact deceleration to the car bolted down on the trolley without damage, meant bodies could be reused.

The fully-equipped car in 30mph barrier test had to finish with the doors being able to open and spilling less

GT crash at 30mph into the block at MIRA caught on high speed film.

complicated rig was designed to enable our cars to be rotated at 90° intervals after the crash and held to ensure no liquids, especially petrol, could leak, even with a full fuel tank.

Making the rollover rig needed channels on rollers and a geared chain drive control. The channels had to be formed in two matching halves and our development engineers found a firm to get them specially made. No other facility like this existed as far as we could see, so it was really a one-off.

In MG development a pendulum was designed to test airbag operation and facia panels using a dummy and, to test bumpers, using a weight equivalent to the car tested with a nose shape as defined by the NHTSA standard.

Kodak high speed filming was used to verify dummy movement and on board UV recorders to show deceleration traces during impact.

In addition rear barrier impact testing was now added to the standard requirements, which involved damage protection to the fuel tanks and piping, exhaust systems and handbrake controls. These were done at MIRA as a proper facility was set up there.

than 1 eggcup full of fuel. A ninety-percentile dummy (NHTSA specification) had to be fully restrained if seat belts were fitted, or suffer only limited deceleration if air bags were installed. The dummy had triaxial sensors in the head and neck which recorded the forces experienced.

Compliance testing to USA Federal Motor Vehicle Standards applied after 1973

The major effect caused by the 30mph impact barrier test was on structural design and passenger safety. A

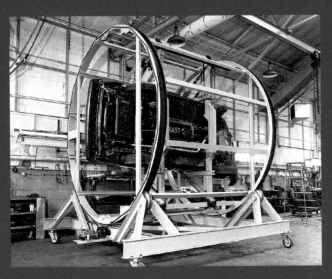

MG rollover test rig in holding car at 90 degrees.

Midget 15mph mobile barrier test at MIRA.

MGB 15mph rear barrier test: the fuel tank deformed but
there was no leak. Shows modified rear brake cable.

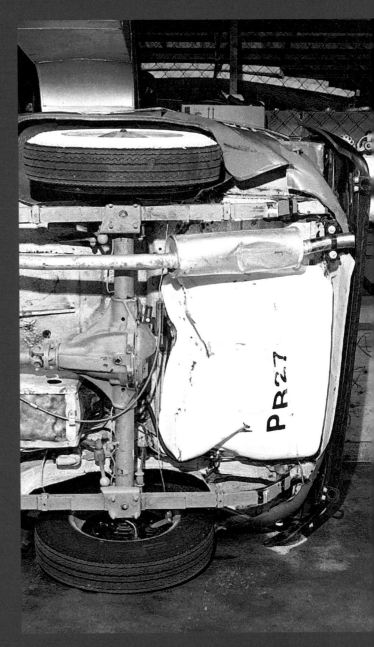

MG 'B' notes

'B' curves

Setting up a body draft for a full-sized proof of the body shapes from quarter-scale requires some basic work. A roll of special cartridge paper is laid out on a wooden table of 18 x 5ft, and pinned securely all round. The surface is then moistened all over with clean water and allowed to dry, which gives a very even tensioned draft.

A high-strength black thread is pinned and pulled tight from one end of the paper to the other, and fine pencil dashes marked along the paper. This allows a straightedge to be used to establish a base line, from which a grid of 10in lines can be drawn very accurately covering the draft.

The next stage is to mark where the front axle or zero line is to be, and a centreline for the plan view and front and rear end views. Then, by scaling up the accurate quarter-scale profiles and curves, the full-size shapes can be developed.

Proving the run of curves involves laying out the car centreline profile, and wing crown lines, wheel openings, and transverse panel curves. Wing curves and side lines, in particular, have highlight lines on sections at 30, 45 and 60 degrees to ensure continuity. (Highlight lines are where reflected light runs along the outside panels from front to rear of the car: in the case of the MGB, starting from the headlamp and following a path to the taillamp. In the paint finish shop, strip lighting is used for this, enabling operators to check that panel surfaces are correct.)

The radiator aperture line is one of the most difficult and most important, in that it controls the styling key to the visible character of the car front on the road. Following the MGA sloping radiator style of 1954 onward – which itself followed the, up to then, traditionally developed vertical MG radiators – was a challenge. The quarter-scale drawing EX 214 enlarged okay, allowing detail shape and new radiator badge profile and centre bar to be eventually fixed.

From the body lines as drawn in pencil, tracings could be taken in all views, using the 10in line grid as reference for the wooden model and pattern makers, so a full-size pattern could be made. Opening lines for doors, bonnet and trunk lid were then constructed, requiring final approval by the planning and tooling engineers when set up on the models. The chassis designers were now able to detail engine and suspension layout. Body structure detail and design was confirmed and initiated.

'B' detail design

Early in the design of new body items such as door locks, hinges for bonnet, door and trunk lids, lamps and mouldings have to be programmed. These may involve special tooling and testing at considerable cost, and therefore Design has to look at whatever is currently available in the organisation or motor trade.

The first proposal was to carry over the MGA door lock with the addition of an outside door handle, since the MGA tourer had an inside door pull cable and the MGA coupé was not suitable.

Supplier to the group Wilmot Breeden was consulted, and found a suitable pullout handle which fitted well on the door shape. This had been developed for a Volkswagen and the tooling paid for. Use by MG was cleared, and I designed a cranked operating lever for the new door handle to operate the existing MGA lock.

This was produced and fitted on the first production, and ran until the change to push-button-type anti-burst locks improved matters. These latter Schonitzer locks were being offered by Wilmot Breedon for other cars, and stayed with the B until production ended.

The door hinges designed at the same time were special swan neck versions needed to fit in the pillar structure, and to suit the door opening panel lines. Bloxwith Lock and Stamping Co came up with a suitable development incorporating a simple spring opening catch function, and this was accepted.

Simple hinges for bonnet and trunk lid were drawn up and fitted, and new versions of the bonnet lock and safety catch were approved.

Standard 8in round headlamps were from Lucas, but unique new sidelamps and flashers were styled to blend in with the new body shapes, particularly at the rear to continue the tail fin lines. Headlamp testing in 1951-2 was simple in that we fitted prototype cars with alternatives, and drove out with the Lucas representatives to find a nice, quiet piece of local road. This road needed to be straight with a slight rise and fall, and marker signs or posts at distances of up to half a mile. A good stretch near MG works was past the Dog House pub on our test route, and also handy for a pint at appropriate times.

Wilmot Breedon showed us a new push-button trunk lid lock of its design relating, I believe, to an idea also suggested for Volvo.

A new rear MG octagon and letters was based on the existing MG Magnette badge, with the curved fitting adjusted to suit the panel.

A removable windscreen was needed so I drew up a single curve glass for simplicity, mounted in an alloy frame with cast alloy aluminium pillars. A prototype was made to compare with earlier exercise schemes, but the style was not right. A redesign with a flatter curve to the centre of the glass with blending cone curves out to the sides was agreed as an improvement. I drew up the new top and bottom rails, and the complicated detail of the pillar castings, which modelmaker Harry Herring reproduced very accurately in hardwood. These models I took to High Duty Alloys in Slough for assessment and quotes to be made in a high-strength aluminium alloy. The quotes were okay and the models were produced, but the anodised finish never quite matched that of the higher purity top and bottom rails.

Early testing & production

During early testing and production a number of problems arose, many unpredictable, such as the new

First press car, with Tim Binnington, MG Show Shop Manager driving, has the problematic original red reflective radiator badge.

radiator badge. A new shield shape was drawn based on the traditional MG radiator centre, carrying the 'MG Octagon.' Quotations were obtained from suppliers, and Lucas Electrical made a new plastic (for the first time) badge in cellulose-type material with the MG and octagon moulded in and coloured from the rear with a red and black background. This was approved by Enever and Thornley for the first production.

Soon after the first cars came onto the road we were contacted by the police, as the red background finish through cellulose showed at night like a red reflector on the front of the car. The badge finish was changed to matt red paint which resolved the problem.

Another comment received – probably as a result of insufficient testing before competition use – was about the door interior waist rails. Enever had specified that we use a clean 'nose' moulding shape around the body compartment cockpit edge, similar to the one he had seen on another car (a Jaguar) across and above the instrument panel. It was logical to carry this on around the door waist and rear cockpit as a protective moulding.

However, comments were made that, in use, although comparatively soft when pressed locally, the moulding created a pressure line across the driver's shoulder muscles on hard cornering. A running change was introduced to provide a wider, smooth, softly-padded area to reduce pressure, very noticeable on longer sustained corners like ex-airfield racing circuits.

The steering wheel rim size and section we used was the result of pressure from owners to accommodate personal preferences. Over the years, several variations were adopted with differing spoke designs. One proposal from Sales Planning was to have wide, flat spokes with tapered slots. This idea was adopted and seemed fine, until we received customer reaction: ladies' bracelet

Early cockpit with round-nose side plastic rails, which were found to cause problems in competitive use.

jewellery became dangerously trapped during steering, and an unidentified police driver got his finger stuck in the slot, causing him some embarrassment.

An early request from drivers was for a way they could quickly and easily identify switch levers for lights, etc, so, in conjunction with Lucas, a cranked, slightly lengthened switch lever was produced for the overdrive switch on the outer end of the facia panel.

In 1962, the original hood design as a packaway system kept the cockpit rear area clear for luggage, with the frame and rail stored in the boot. The front rail – which clipped to the windscreen top – had to be very stiff, and was designed to provide a water seal at speed. Earlier MGs and other makes had always suffered from water ingress along the top rail, and Enever was determined this should not happen again. The centre spoke rod joining the windscreen lower rail to the top rail was intended to prevent the centre lifting under wind suction. With the centre rod approved, a mirror mounting that clamped onto the rod was drawn up and a sample made, which allowed mirror position to be altered to driver preference.

Tools and jack

During the process of setting up the 'B' for road use, determining tools and spares, etc, the provision of a jack was assessed. A central jacking point under the sill was designed, and a suitable jack obtained, allowing easy access for the driver to operate it. Operation was checked to give full wheel lift clearance on normal cambered roads, and that the car was stable with a wheel removed.

Development boss Alec Hounslow was watching events. He sat on the sill top with the door open, and rocked from side to side to check movement of the car when on the jack. Nothing unexpected happened until it was realised that the jacking tube under the sill was pushed up into and deforming the lower sill section. Alec's additional weight was too much for it – the extra test was validated.

Chassis Design did a rapid rethink and added an internal support bracket inside the sill section that joined up with the floor crossmember. When it retested okay, this was added for first production.

V8 Coventry Climax engine

During various continuing dialogues between Syd and Geoff Healey at Warwick, the pair investigated the installation of a V8 Coventry Climax engine in an MGB GT. Syd took me up to the Cape and we looked at a prototype. This unit fitted well but had the same problem as our final set-up for the Rover 3½-litre engine: there was barely enough operating clearance between

pipes and chassis frame for the run of the exhaust manifold and pipe because of the narrow width between the chassis, and constraint by the front suspension crossmember attachments. I understood that, later, they got the car running but no programme was developed from this.

We also saw the same engine being installed and finalised in the Le Mans Coupé proposal. (See ADO 52 MGC chapter.)

The 'B' in production

From 1959 it was quite a thing to have worked first on all quarter-scale models, then prototypes and development exercises, to actually seeing finished, painted cars in various colours beginning to fill the production lines and export car parks. Naturally enough, designers were always being asked: "How do you expect us to assemble these bits?" "Can we have this part first or after these fixings?" Many minor modifications to parts and parts lists were issued, with the Buying Department ordering revised parts and fairly soon smoothing the production process and the first specially-finished show cars were allocated to the MG Show Shop.

Boss of the Show Shop, Tim Binnington, was ready for the first MGB debut at the 1962 Earls Court Motor Show in London. This entailed selecting bodies with perfect (or nearly!) panel alignment and consistent door and joint gaps. In the 'old days,' as a carryover from coachbuild standards, it should have been possible to roll a half-crown coin right round the panel gaps with little variation in fit. Mass production methods and standards since have tended to allow larger clearances.

Paint finish was important and kerbside 'orange peel' texture (normal production imperfections) was not allowed. Every body in the new paint plant at Bodies

Branch was rubbed down by hand over the primed surfaces, using lots of water with wet-and-dry 'emery' paper, so the operators had to wear rubber aprons and boots.

Introduction of the 'B' – with production intended to exceed that of the MGA and, indeed, all previous models – necessitated a new £1,000,000 paint plant to be built next to the body shop.

As I remember it, the MGB's first introduction was not accompanied by fanfare or great publicity, and the early cars ran around Abingdon on test and delivery without camouflage. The press and motoring magazines had been briefed in outline, and honoured a tacit agreement not to publish in advance. On this basis, journalists were allowed good access, and loan of

The first colour picture agreed for press release in 1962, which was similar to 'Susan Tuck' pre-war pictures.

early cars for their own launch issues. I remember that a foreign (French?) magazine photographer was spotted in Marcham Road on our test circuit. He was apparently accompanied by a devastatingly attractive girl, who was intended to act as a distraction so that the snapper could get some scoop pictures of the new model. Difficult though it was for some of our drivers, the ploy didn't succeed!

It was very gratifying for John Thornley and Syd Enever, a little later, when the 'B' was awarded 'Car of the Year' by Canadian journalists and their trade association. The trophy was a stylised steering wheel, suitably inscribed, which pleased us all no end. Syd passed this on to me to hold for the office when I became Chief Engineer, and it now has a home in the MG Car Club headquarters at Abingdon. We also got a good write-up in *Road & Track,* which was good for the American market where many of the first cars were sold.

Bodies Branch & MG bodies supply

In 1956 Morris Motors Bodies Branch at Quinton Road, Coventry had supplied the MGA body assembly, and Morris Minor Estate Car rear shell assemblies. Its Experimental Department produced the full-size MGB wooden model pattern, and the first all-steel body-in-white assembly. Pressings were ordered from Pressed Steel Swindon to enable production to start.

Every MGB shell was hand-cleaned of oil, hand-sprayed with red oxide primer, and finally hand-sanded all over with wet-and-dry paper. Final paint surfacer and colour was applied, and the body transferred to the assembly shop for trimming, windscreen and hood fitting.

A new paint shop to support this work was approved by Mr Harriman, and paint supplier ICI proposed a new dip tank for the primer process. The body was to be immersed to above the bulkhead level, and panels above that line to be hand-sprayed. The primed body was mechanically line-controlled to drop into the primer vat, and then climb a ramp to enable surplus paint to drain off through body holes provided for this purpose. This worked well apart from a witness edge-of-paint line that was left, particularly on the bonnet. The hand-spraying did not cover well, so every panel had to be hand-sanded to feather the paint edge. This was an absolute MG first! We had allowed for this with suitable air escape holes, and paint drainage in the floors and sills.

ICI suggested deepening the primer vat to submerge the whole body, and this was done. Paint representatives and management gathered to watch the first body through the revised process. It came down into the primer but, due to the trapped air in the upper panels, floated off the mechanical line hooks, which moved on alone, leaving the body to slowly and gracefully sink to the bottom of the vat. Not much was said and we all left, leaving Bill Bailly and the Planning Department with a difficult submarine recovery operation ...

A suitable clip restraint to enable bodyshell positive location was introduced, and all MGBs had this treatment until final body welding and painting processes were transferred to Pressed Steel at Cowley.

Development for racing & rallying

In late 1962, as cars became available, Competitions began to look at possible development of the 'B' in racing and rallying, the first occasion being an entry in the USA Sebring event.

This was the first time that any tuning for performance had been done on the new 'B' series engine. Two cars were prepared, but testing was severely held up at Finmere airfield by snow and ice on the road and test circuits. In the event, the long, high-speed airfield corners at Sebring caused oil surge in the sump, leading to big end and main bearing failure, and a 'Did not finish.' Sump baffle redesign was quickly on the cards, and the resulting unit built into all later MGB engines.

An entry for Le Mans – a higher speed circuit – prompted Syd Enever to begin a design project for a streamlined nose shape for the car, and a new alloy front end was drawn up and produced. Syd estimated this would give another 5-6mph, and 7 DBL was timed at over 130mph, winning the 2-litre class against competing Porsches and Lotuses. The same car was entered at Le Mans again in 1964, driven by Paddy Hopkirk and Andrew Hedges, and timed at nearly 140mph on the Mulsanne straight, winning the 'Best British Car' trophy.

Long-nose-style MGB for Le Mans.

Changes: 1964 onward

In late 1964, Longbridge design had provided a new 5-bearing 'B' series engine for our MG production at Abingdon. This caused some changes in the tunnel and floor due to relocation of the starter motor, which also moved the foot-operated dip switch. A whole series of changes to improve operation and cost were implemented, such as the greater capacity pressed fuel tank, and anti-burst door locks in line with the MG Midget.

Another significant change which involved much testing with suppliers were radial ply tyres in place of cross-ply, with consequent improvement in ride and handling.

By 1965 we had been scheming and drawing new coupé roof shapes, increasing windscreen height, and altering the rear end. None of the lines and models were quite right, and Syd accompanied John Thornley to the Italian car show to evaluate new styles.

While there, in discussion with Farina, it was agreed that MG would provide a tourer from production for Farina to propose a new coupé shape. A prototype, painted lime green, was delivered to MG, and was immediately viewed and approved by the directors. A copy of the Farina body lines draft was obtained and, apart from minor changes to ease production of the quarterlight hinges and the trunk lid supports, was drawn and issued to Pressed Steel Swindon. Production was authorised and scheduled for October 1965. New windscreen, door, and backlight glasses were detailed for suppliers, and the associated sealing rubbers and finishers – including door quarterlights, new child seat, rear carpets and trim – were issued.

What Farina did by increasing windscreen height, and providing a large trunk lid with the crisp break line

Farina prototype MGB GT delivered for director viewing and approval of raised windscreen and new roof line with hatchback.

along the roof edges, produced a completely new style for the MGB. John Thornley was happy in that he now had our own version of a town car (the poor man's Aston Martin.)

1974 European legislation effects

Following the backing given to vehicle safety by various European governments, involvement in exhibitions and research, and noise testing became important.

One particular market for MG was Switzerland, where altitude had an effect on compliance with noise regulation standards. An exercise was set up to test a known engineering GT MGB in Zurich, and deduce whether local fitting of sound-deadening materials would improve on the 84 decibel level which was about normal for production cars. I arranged for Steve Gray – one of

Alec Hounslow's Development Engineers – and myself to drive our car to Zurich to our British Leyland distributor, and test on the spot. We arranged at the same time with the helpful Swiss test authority through Keller's, the MG sales agent, to have the authority test and hopefully award advance approval, at the local height above sea level recorded at Zurich.

Testing was carried out on an isolated local road, both stationary and drive-by, at fixed speeds and rpm, which proved we were just over the noise limit. Back at the distributor we fitted sound-deadening composite felts under the bonnet, and on the wheelarches, and retested, only just complying by equalling the required 84db. Several variations were tried but without marked improvement. The implication was that a much more controlled exhaust system was needed and, since we did not have anything locally available, we had to return to the factory.

A redesigned system was obtained from Radiators Branch with better silencer packing, and sent out for re-test. This gave us compliance for another year, but further reduction in noise levels meant that, without engine noise reduction by redesign for a limited market, withdrawal from Switzerland would be the only option.

One day we were testing the GT on open roads near Zurich – necessary because no suitable test facility was available. We were getting consistent results on the noise meter on a quiet valley road at 6am in the morning – no traffic – when we noticed unusual peaks on the readout. Looking round and listening – nothing apparent – until over the rise came an almost silent electric milk delivery van, bottles clinking ...

The Swiss authority's tester accepted interim proof of compliance, but needed more official approval as our figures were only just okay.

GT in Zurich altitude test with meters set up on valley road.

Incidentally, for some Swiss owners, distributor Emil Frey had set up a line to wax spray the underside of Japanese cars, then being imported. MGBs sold at the same time got the treatment – as a bonus! This type of underspraying with a wax-oil liquid was approved and could be done as an extra by distributors as MG had no space or line facility.

Sebring GT MGBs

A red MGB GT, registered by Competitions LBL 591 E, was entered for Sebring 1967 in the GT class as a prototype. It had a bored out racing engine of 2004cc and was driven driven by Paddy Hopkirk and Andrew Hedges to 11th place – 1st in class.

The car was shipped back to England but was badly damaged at the docks – both front chassis legs were bent so the car was stripped and the body (only) eventually sold to Robin Vokins, a comps mechanic. This body had been repaired and straightened, and checked on a CKD jig at Cowley – with no engine and no papers – then stored.

For Sebring 1968 another GT – in green, this time, using the same number LBL 591E transferred from the original red car – was prepared by Competitions. This was driven by an all-American crew of C Rodrigues, R McDaniel, and D Brack, and was 18th in class.

After some time, the original red car was purchased from Robin Vokins by Bob Neville, who rebuilt it and got the DVLA (UK registration authority) to reissue its number LBL 591E when original records were produced for it. This is still in England and owned and run by Mike D'Arcy.

The differences between these two cars can be verified from original records of the chassis numbers. I understand from Bob that Dougie Watts and John Dale were involved in helping with his rebuild, and also on the 1968 car.

MGB frontal styling: complaint from Renault

At the end of 1962, four months after the MGB had gone into production, Morris Motors received a complaint from Renault that the frontal design of its Caravelle had been 'copied' by MG. The design registration was dated 13-7-59 for the Caravelle and Floride models, the particular area claimed as unique being the headlamp pockets on the bonnet and front wing.

Correspondence between A H Steed, patent agent for BMC, and Syd Enever for MG, was carefully followed by Alec Issigonis. The correspondence stated that MG design and styling drawings of the panel shapes in question, for which models existed, were dated earlier than the Renault design registration date of 13-7-59. Publications also existed showing recessed headlamp treatments, and were published in France, Germany, Italy, USA and the UK. Some of these designs did have glass or plastic streamlined covers but were thought to be relevant by Cabinet Lavoix, Renault's legal

representatives in Paris, who became involved. They wrote to Mr Steed and, after making comparisons of the designs, did not positively support the Renault case. One of the points clarified during the correspondence was that MG was owned by Morris Motors.

A final letter from Morris (Mr Steed), dated 26 November 1963, notified Issigonis and Enever that Renault had decided to drop the matter. It also advised MG to check styling comparisons in the future.

During design of the MGB front, I was familiar with the appearance of other sports cars, such as those by Ferrari, Maserati, and Mercedes. However, the MGB evolved by taking on the rounded aerofoil shape of EX 181, and Jim O'Neill's ideas for a new car, both of which entailed keeping the headlamps as far back and close to the front wheels as possible. The series of quarter-scale models I drew to gradually arrive at the B came from Jim's drawing dated 28.6.57 and mine of 9.6.58 – EX 214/1 up to ADO 23/163 – quarter-scale MGB/2 dated 1.5.59 with the final radiator grille shape. I think this proved there was no outside influence in the model's design, and all of the drawings went as evidence to the patent office.

It did, however, highlight that UK registration of car design in general did not exist, and had to be considered.

American recall

During early sales of the first production 1975 model year cars in the USA, our American Leonia staff were told that the Government Testing Department had bought and tested an MGB. The car was involved in a 5mph barrier test which it failed, to such an extent that the engine had moved forward during impact and the fan had damaged the radiator – potentially causing a leak. The implication of this was that any MGB in this series could fail in a similar road accident, and therefore a modification (if possible) was to be made on all future cars, with those already sold recalled and updated.

Since we had done a similar test before release without failure, we needed to verify the American test system and results. I arranged with Leonia management to visit the Agbabian test laboratory near Los Angeles with one of our Development Engineers.

We quickly flew out, met up with Graham Gardner, our American engineer, and went to the lab to see the tested car and the test facility. They had been very professional and the car was correctly set up, so we had to accept the failure and look for a solution.

A second small recorded failure was that testers found that the taillamp lens fixing screws were loose and bent: caused by the test crash? This seemed to me highly unlikely, and I asked for a second repeat test in front of us. This they agreed to do, and we watched them set up the car and push it onto the ramp for the start of the test. We noted that staff pushed the car by hand, with two men bearing on the taillamp lens, and it was this that caused the lens to move and deflect, bending the screws! The screw failure was promptly removed from the failure list with apologies and red faces on their part.

A recall was accepted by us, and we returned to MG to arrange modifications to increase clearance between the fan and the radiator, as an interim measure. Design decided to move the radiator forward to the 'C' and V8 position with electric fans, thus obviating the old engine-mounted fan, and we added an engine restraint bar from the gearbox bellhousing bottom to the chassis crossmember for all future cars. This was the last significant engineering change unique to American and Canadian LHD cars.

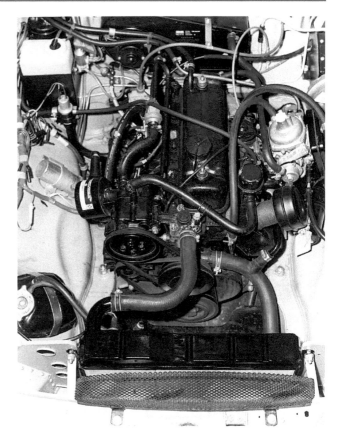

MGB engine with radiator moved to forward position in order to pass American 5mph barrier test.

Alterations & improvements
During the production life of the 'B,' apart from legislated changes and improvements, Design was approached by industry suppliers with possible alternatives and improvements. Wheels and tyres were changing, and testing was done on sports tyres, including

the short-term Dunlop Duraband and several alloy wheel designs. Competitions, alongside us, kept pressure on for suitable race track and rally handling developments, underlining the idea that "Racing improves the Breed."

Through our distributors' knowledge of the wider North American market. Feedback from Australia, now with its own production facility, and the knock-down assemblies in South Africa and New Zealand kept production up-to-date. The desire of MG owners to personalise their cars has always had an influence on the marque, and long may this continue.

Production parts history

Owners may be interested to know that the steel sheets from which the car panels were pressed may have crossed the Atlantic at least twice.

In the 1960s, supplies of low carbon sheet were in short supply in Europe, and coils were obtained from Bethlehem Steel in the USA in OHSPEDDO (Open Hearth, Single Pickled, Extra Deep Drawing, Oiled) at 16, 18 and 20 gauge for wings, sills, and other deep pressings. This steel gave a good surface when formed, and was very suitable for spot welding and roller welding to provide a strong body structure. Sample welds were tested regularly in the laboratory, particularly on chassis joints and sills.

Special cars!

I was once approached at a Silverstone MG meeting by an American lady, who had learned of my connection with the 'B' from the B Register desk. Asked whether I saw all the cars on the production line, I replied "Yes." Oh good, she said, do you remember mine? It was the yellow one! Completely flummoxed, I had to say, sorry, not specifically out of 180 a day! Her car was so special to her that she assumed it was special when first completed and shipped over to the USA for her to buy. It would be nice to think that the system could have been made to work that way!

Competition cars are very different because they develop a history once allocated to a driver and events. Years later, when these cars stop competing and are sold to private owners, queries arise as to authenticity. Most can be correctly identified as their original build and specification set-up would have been by a particular comps mechanic, who had his own unique way of drilling holes, bending pipes, fitting brackets, and recording data. Many disputes about history have been resolved by reference to this.

Alec Hounslow's retirement presentation, which took place in front of the Design and Development team and the V8 tyre test prototype.

My own contact with historical records for development cars over twenty years was in getting the book for each car updated and maintained. Alec Hounslow, the boss, had every car book on file in his office, with lots of the old ones stored in a wooden tea chest under his desk. This chest, for him on his one-off fabricated 'K' type racing seat mounted on a steel tube frame, still in original green leather, was a footrest.

Under Triumph management, when Alec retired, Barry Trewin took over locally, though overall control was at Longbridge under John Turnbull.

At the end, with the Acclaim programme moved to Cowley, Cliff Bray was instructed to move only modern records to Morris at Cowley, and put everything else in the skip, which is where all old Development car records went. There was no chance to save anything. How sad ...

MG production line: (left to right) Syd Enever, retired Chief Engineer, on a visit, Don Hayter, Chief Engineer, Terry Mitchell, Chief Chassis Draughtsman, and Jim O'Neill, Chief Body Engineer.

The Austin Healey Sprite & MG Midget

During 1956-7, Geoffrey and Brian Healey, in the old cinema building in Warwick, started a brand new small sports car project.

This was based on the Austin A35 using a twin carburetter version of the A series engine, with a unique body but some carryover suspension parts on new underframe pressings. The original idea was for flip-up headlamps, which did not reach production as they were not completely developed.

The Austin Healey 100 was already being produced at Longbridge, and Donald Healey got approval from Leonard Lord for the Austin design office to originate Sprite body production drawings. From these, tooling and pressings were made ready for assembly at the factory. However, production line space was not available as the Issigonis Mini was under way, so the decision was made to use the MG factory, where capacity was available. All design information was transferred to MG Design and Development under Syd Enever, with chassis pressings from Thompsons being delivered to Pressed Steel Swindon for assembly on bodies built there. From Swindon the complete shell went to Cowley for paint and on to the Abingdon production line. Production was scheduled for early 1958.

As a direct result of the change in location no development results from prototype or production assembly car conditions were available to MG Design, which could only begin full testing as the first cars came off the production line.

The MG development test for prototypes and major

Sprite prototype on development road test.

structural changes required 500 miles on the Pavé circuit at the MIRA facility near Nuneaton. For our mechanics this entailed a 180 mile round trip from MG every morning, then a day's driving on the Pavé. We also used the ride and handling circuit for durability tests, as well as the brake test strip. Each car was run weighted for driver and passenger, full fuel tank, and a 35lb weight on the luggage grid fitted on the boot panel.

Since the Sprite had quarter-elliptic rear suspension – the entire rear loads behind the heelboard and wheel – arches were overhung.

Early Pavé results revealed that the rear body structure was failing, and even the prototype I was using on the road every day to go to and from Coventry showed creasing on the outer rear wing panel between the door opening and rear wheelarch. Production was immediately halted and a repair reinforcing scheme introduced with handmade parts initially. Some of the steel panel thicknesses were slightly increased and modifications issued.

New Sprite front end and grille style: unchanged rear.

MG Midget rear end, with new trunk lid, on the Sprite. It was
Enever's decision to use my MGB tail fin and lamps.

For the first time an MG production line went into reverse, removing all affected trim items and mechanical parts. New and modified parts were welded in and, with fingers and legs crossed, testing restarted to achieve the necessary performance level. All-in-all a very hectic period, but the improved car ran for about 18 months until the Mk2 arrived.

Unusual production conditions included problems accessing the underneath of the rear of the engine compartment with the rear-hinged bonnet, and accessing the tail lamps wiring with no trunk lid. In the summer on our top deck production lines, this latter difficulty meant having to glue-in the rear trunk carpets whilst working in the same area, also climbing in to make tail lamp wiring connections. Workers were nodding off mid-job, and complaining of the fumes, so a quick change to a new, low toxic adhesive called MG Plus was necessitated, after clearance to establish safety.

We in Development were already testing the increased power, Healey-proposed A series, and the then new diaphragm clutch from Lockheed. I took a prototype down to Cornwall on an extended holiday run. By the time I was on the way home the clutch was already slipping on acceleration, and I only just crept home over the railway bridge. I had to wait for gaps in the traffic to nurse it in to MG next morning. An improved clutch design resolved the fault.

During 1960, Brian Healey had produced a revised version of the Sprite, with a more conventional front wing and bonnet, though still retaining the original rear end. At MG Syd had begun a new rear end using my MGB tail fins and lamp design, with a trunk lid giving access to the rear luggage compartment. With approval from Harriman, the two designs were amalgamated for the Sprite and the new MG Midget was born. New

Final Midget, with side chrome strips, which was run with the MG1 number plate transferred from an MGA twin cam.

radiator shapes and chrome mouldings ensured separate identities, together with new wheel finish discs and colour schemes. As agreed between Healey and MG Design, the rear suspension was changed from quarter-elliptic to semi-elliptic springs, obviating the old torque arms and simplifying the structure, and providing improved control and suspension movement on the axle.

Subsequent product changes were wind-up windows, a new windscreen, different seats and trim, and increased engine capacity from 998cc to 1098cc,

and eventually the 1275cc A series engine as also used in the Mini-Cooper. The front brakes were also uprated to Lockheed discs, and tyre sizes increased.

With further minor styling improvements, Sprite and Midget continued through until the start of the American 'Safe at any Speed' crash-related safety changes in the early 1970s.

The advent of the American Federal Safety Standard in 1974-5 required all cars to pass the 30mph crash test, and the pendulum test, which involves swinging a

1964 Midget, now with wind-up windows.

specified nose shape (equivalent in weight to that of the car) onto the bumper of the car under test; also tighter emission limits specified. Similarly to the MGB, the ride height of the MG Midget had to be increased so that no damage to lights or engine and mechanical operations occurred under test. Triumph Engineering was now in charge of design, and Harry Webster, Director, and John Lloyd decided to use the Spitfire 1500cc engine in the Midget and Sprite. This change meant that the cars' weight put them in the same emission class, with common testing. Triumph design modified the Spitfire, and Harris Mann at Longbridge, in the old Austin styling studio, provided the Midget and Sprite rubber bumper based on the MGB channel structure.

Terry Mitchell in MG Chassis Design did the new engine installation, and, as instructed, changed the gearbox to the Austin Marina type. Development obtained test engines from Triumph, and built prototypes for road testing with changed axle ratios to allow for increased horsepower and weight. The additional horsepower from the bigger engine was going to make the Midget slightly faster, if a little heavier, so a change in rear axle ratio was necessary.

Two problems showed up, however. Firstly, the performance and high-speed testing produced big end failure quite quickly. Investigation revealed that big end and main bearing finish on the crankshafts was not good enough. Triumph examined the methods for the final finish and agreed to improve quality to inside 15 microns, as well as to supply more engines.

Secondly, the water flow through the engine block was not adequate when compared with the Midget's usual water pump and radiator system. A larger crossflow radiator was obtained, and increased flow achieved, which provided the necessary improvement for the cooling tests.

At the same time, crash testing at 30mph and pendulum weight tests revealed that some body improvements were needed. The change in engine and gearbox also required a change to the engine restraint and mountings in order to pass the 5mph barrier 'no damage' test.

Extended road testing followed in parallel with laboratory emission testing, which showed compliance, but the similarity in weight class of the Triumph Spitfire and MG Midget required accurate recording of weights during production, and continuos monitoring. An accurate drive-on-and-off weight platform with a covered tunnel was installed next to Design and Development. As mentioned previously, leaving the doors of the tunnel open for access resulted in unacceptable weight variations, due to the windflow in the tunnel having enough aerodynamic effect to give unreliable figures. Shutting the doors at each end resolved the problem at the expense of considerably slowing the process.

NHTSA crash tests also called for rear end impact testing. In parallel with the MGB, Midgets had to withstand the rear end mobile barrier test at 20mph, in fully loaded condition, and with a full fuel tank, without any spillage either during or after the test. Initial tests at MIRA showed damage to the tank caused by the handbrake pivot on the rear axle. Changes to the handbrake cable, fuel lines, and carbon canister

Midget on rollover test set-up after barrier test.

breathing system on the engine were designed and tested before successful passes were obtained.

The final test involved rotating the car successively through 90, 180 and 270 degrees after the test crash with no spillage.

Other changes affecting cars for the USA market were the collapsable steering column, and the addition of engine restraint cables, both of which combined to increase overall weight, though the biggest weight change had been the rubber bumper (moulded polyurethane-on-steel double channels) at each end, which actually improved ride if not the handling.

The American market was slower to accept and purchase these cars, modified to comply with Californian emissions and durability standards. This caused Triumph and Austin to concentrate on new models such as the Lynx and a new MG, neither of which went into production.

Sprite & Midget notes

Midget replacement ADO34 and EX 234

Until 1954 the name Midget had been used only with the TF in its final form with a 1500cc engine. Initially, the completely new MGA 1500cc was called Midget but this was changed when John Thornley said "Call it MGA" and the alphabet sequence was restarted.

In 1958, Donald Healey reached agreement with the Austin Longbridge directors that they would finalise drawings and produce the ADO13 Sprite. Finding production line space was a problem, and Abingdon was finishing the Magnette and Pathfinder, so all details were transferred to MG for production to start. This involved the introduction of an integral pressed steel platform chassis, and gave added gravitas to MG Abingdon's production history.

At the same time the ADO 15 Mini Minor was going into production, and, with its separate front and rear subframes on a steel bodyshell, gave rise to a new trend in sports cars.

At Longbridge, Jack Daniels, working directly for Alec Issigonis, had designed the production panels and frames for the Mini. In 1958, he drew up a floor platform structurally linking the front and rear chassis frames of a Mini Cooper version as an ADO34 sports version, which was sent to Italy to have a Farina light alloy bodyshell designed and fitted. A hard top roof was also supplied.

Meanwhile, at Abingdon, Enever was aware of this, and decided to design and build his own version using ADO34 MG and ADO35 Austin Healey numbers, but utilising a minivan platform with slightly longer 84in wheelbase. The body was styled in parallel with the now developed MGB final shapes with inset headlamp

ADO34 Mini subframe-based sports by Jack Daniels for Alec Issigonis. Body styled and built by Frua in Italy.

pockets and rear tail fins and lamps. This was built and development-tested on the road, but the lack of roof stiffening structure caused an unacceptable 'scuttle shake' so the model was finally scrapped as it was felt the floor structure could not be effectively stiffened to carry the Mini subframing.

In 1961 the new midget ADO47 version of the Sprite, now designated ADO41, was in production, and Enever was having further thoughts about suspension related to hydrolastic units and the Mini's bigger brother the ADO16. In 1962 a Sprite was modified to use interconnected front and rear hydrolastic units with a rear adjustable anti-roll bar system. This was road tested and, in conjunction with Competitions, assessed by Timo Makinen and other drivers, who got favourable results.

Roy Brocklehurst was given a clean sheet of paper on which to design a new platform chassis frame for a Midget EX234, using this suspension and a tuned A series 1275cc engine. Two chassis were made in MG

ADO35 Mini van-based with 84in wheelbase. Enever specified an MG sports car as a possible replacement for the FWD Midget.

Development, and the first was sent to Italy for the Farina factory to make a running prototype for MG. This was done and returned to Abingdon for assessment, and representing a huge jump forward in styling and seating and body package. As this was a one-off no road testing or development work was carried out.

Investment in MG body alternatives was strictly limited, with possible Triumph new models being considered and the 'O' series ADO21 programme now on the drawing board.

MG Midget coupés – Dick Jacobs
In 1962 when private owners were beginning to use the Midget in competition, Dick Jacobs – who already had a team of MGAs – became interested in the idea,

and approached John Thornley and Syd Enever with the suggestion they make a Midget coupé suitable for Sebring, Le Mans, and other circuit races. Syd agreed and a new lightweight body was drawn up by Jim O'Neill and Denis Williams based on the production chassis. Lines and details for a model were quickly developed and three bodies in alloy were ordered from Midland Sheet Metal, near Coventry. When completed they came to Abingdon Experimental/Development shop for installation of racing seats, instruments, special engines and fuel tanks.

Two cars were for Dick Jacobs and one for John Milne, and initial testing was controlled by Alec Hounslow with Tom Haig driving.

The roof shape of the coupé was a combination,

EX 234 MG prototype had a new chassis platform with hydrolastic suspension and body by Farina of Italy.

at Dick's request, to achieve lines similar to that of the Aston Martin DB4, and lines which I had already drawn for an MGB coupé. Combined with a new streamlined front end and bonnet shape, this gave improved wind tunnel performance and top speed potential. These cars eventually ran with great success in the international GT class at Brands Hatch, Silverstone, Goodwood and Sebring.

Coincidentally, I had drawn the first DB4 roof shapes for David Brown and Frank Feeley while at Feltham in 1955. They, naturally, stuck in my mind for the MGB, so Jim and Denis achieved a very nice smaller version of this for the Midget.

The cars still exist in the Beer Collection at Houghton near Huntingdon.

Big Healeys

In early 1956, production of the first six-cylinder Healey 3000 began at Longbridge, but George Harriman authorised its transfer to MG at Abingdon almost straight away as the cessation of Riley production had left line capacity there.

Bodies were built by Jensen at Smethwick, the latest 2912cc, six-cylinder engines and gearbox came from Morris Engines, and suspension parts from BMC Tractors and Transmissions.

Alec Hounslow, under Syd Enever's guidance, started development testing, and Marcus Chambers began assessment for competition use. Brian Healey and the team from Warwick continued with their own competition cars for rallies and liaison with development at Abingdon.

When the BN6 Healey was in production at Abingdon, various problems arose. Once the body, as delivered from Jenson was put on the line, the big six engine and gearbox were lowered in, but the weight caused the body and chassis to bend so that the doors no longer fitted nicely to the locks, necessitating a reset operation.

While this and other problems were corrected, Jensen Design, under Kevin Beattie and Eric Neale, was developing improvements on the body, including wind-up windows, and new seats and trim. Development mechanics had also found that, in fully loaded condition and parked on a roadside camber, it was not easy to get the jack in position with a flat tyre on that side. Competitions used higher springs and a different jack to overcome this.

The last version was the BJ8, which ran for about a year until production at Abingdon ceased.

All of the racing and rally development was done in Competitions, first under Stuart Turner and then Peter Browning, with considerable success.

MGC – ADO 52

Original ideas for a larger, possibly 3-litre MG Sports Saloon began with a scheme by Chassis Design on which a body shape was drawn by Jim O'Neill. A quarter-scale model of this was made in Development, while engine possibilities were evaluated in EX 210.

At the same time first plans for an MGA replacement were being drawn, early engine projects for which included a 3-litre V6 engine and some early work on this allowed for its installation in a coupé.

Alec Issigonis had in mind a new, six-cylinder engine as a development of the Austin 3-litre saloon. Information from BMC Australia indicated that its new, lightweight, 2.6-litre six-cylinder version was possibly available.

Syd got an engine, already developed, from BMC Australia, and set up a small design section in the boiler house, employing Pat Rees from Gerry Palmer's Cowley office to design a special, based on the MGB chassis and body. Pat designed a new tubular front suspension crossmember with torsion bar springing, and an engine and gearbox installation. Parts were fabricated, an early 'B' chassis was modified, and a prototype built.

Road testing went well with a top speed of just under 130mph. The new Oxford southern bypass was open, and Roy Brocklehurst and Tom Haig were timed by Oxford police testing their new speed-checking equipment. When stopped they were asked "What have you got under the bonnet? That was 127mph. Please be careful!" No maximum speed limit then!

No further work was done on this specification as the Australian engine did not become available.

Longbridge Engine Design, under Issigonis, was well on with the 3-litre, and Syd got a copy of the design outline block and head so that Roy and Terry Mitchell could do an installation to compare with Pat

Quarter-scale Jim O'Neill design for big MG Coupé (EX 210).

Quarter-scale Don Hayter design for big MG Coupé (EX 210). The new twin headlamp scheme was by Lucas.

Rees' Australian prototype MGB. Syd decided that the Issigonis design was too tall, with too long a stroke for a free-revving engine, and proposed a change to Issigonis. This was rejected out of hand!

We eventually got the Austin 3-litre engine and made an MGC version of the 'B.' The longer, six-cylinder block fitted with a new increased size radiator moved forward inside a modified bonnet-locking platform. A power bulge was needed in the bonnet with a clearance bulge also for the front carburettor dashpot.

A new front crossmember and torsion bar mountings were joined to new sidemembers and wheelarch side panels. Development testing showed high under-bonnet temperatures, and additional holes were tried above the bulkhead through to vents out of the front wings at the side. Similarly, extra electric fan extraction was tried. Finally, with a new larger engine fan and larger deeper radiator the problem was solved with both 2 and 3 carburettor versions.

MGC sales demonstrator in the new MG sales and shipping compound.

When Competitions was looking for rally developments, it asked for a light alloy engine in a GT body. Since another big change had been to 15in wheels, Comps specified alloy rims, and minilite specials were obtained. The bigger tyre sections needed wing eyebrows to provide legally required body cover width. I had already arranged for alloy wings for the MGB to be made at Swindon, but even wider versions were needed.

Stuart Turner – Comps Manager – and Syd agreed to go further, and special GT bodies were made using light alloy exterior panels. This necessitated joining the roof and quarter panels, pressed in alloy, to the steel inner reinforcements with rivets and special glue. Six panels sets were specially pressed and hand-worked to final assembly, and completed bodies painted for supply to Competitions for entry in Sebring. The large eyebrow wing extensions were drawn by Eric Carter, and patterns made and sent to Midland Sheet Metal to be made by hand. These were then welded on to the suitably modified MGB alloy wing pressings, ready for assembly at the same time.

Pressed Steel Swindon used to reset the wing press tools and run small sets in heavier gauge alloy for the MGB, and some of these were further modified by Midland Sheet Metal to provide the big eyebrows hand-worked for the GT Specials.

The first C to really run in this form – with a B bonnet – had to use a bored-out MGB engine at 2 litres, as not enough bodies were made for homologation. This car was by now up against very special Porsches, Lancias and Ferraris, so no chance of a win except in the more limited 2-litre class in the Targa Florio.

A car was entered and a team of Competitions mechanics went out to set up practice and evaluate

MGC GTS special-bodied competition car.

the circuit. It and other teams hired local cars to drive around to prepare navigators' notes for the race. Our mechanics noticed that other teams were putting green and red paint marks on posts and rocks just before tight corners to help their drivers. This seemed a good idea, so they did some of their own and later, on the quiet, changed and deleted some of the opposition's! The car achieved 12th overall, 4th in category.

The Publicity Department tried to increase the market with various high-profile MGC models, a notable example being the MGC GT that MG Production built for Prince Charles. University Motors did the 2+2 version with more expensive trim, and Comps finally got the all-alloy engine, though too late. During this period the automatic Borg Warner 35 gearbox, which was on the 1795cc, four-cylinder, and had continued to be developed, became the unit most suitable for the big 6 version.

ADO 51: Healey version of MGC

Following the design of the larger engined version of the MGB into the MGC, Product Planning proposed a Healey badge-engineered package. Syd agreed that MG Design could style a Healey radiator intake and grille, use different side mouldings and wheel trims, and provide restyled, high-class interior trim and seats. This we did, and produced a prototype with hand-made chromium-plated parts, styled to suit, on a special body in Healey blue.

A directors' viewing was scheduled, but the idea was completely turned down by Donald Healey, as the directors already had other ideas. Geoffrey Healey had a Rolls-Royce 4-litre engine installed in a wider version of the Big Healey as a new model. Donald, we were informed, did not want one of their cars based on an MG, although he had earlier accepted an MG based on the Sprite.

The prototype was converted back to a standard MGC, and used for development tests; the programme was shelved.

P76 Australian saloon testing

In around 1976-77, Austin-Rover management was in discussion with BMC, Australia, about development of its new P76 saloon. BMC did not have suitable test facilities available, so it was decided to send a car with Development Engineer Ross Weber to England where MG could provide workshop space in Development with mechanics and test drivers to run a programme. This also allowed access to the road handling circuit and brake test and Pave strip at MIRA, plus motorway and cross-country roads.

The P76 was a large saloon with trailing arm coil spring rear suspension, and panhard rod location intended to give a comfortable ride in the Australian outback.

The engine was the developed light six unit designed and built in BMC's factory, and was essentially the same as the one obtained by Enever previously. It was used in the prototype MGC (ADO 52).

A section of Development was allocated to the work, with mechanics and drivers transferred when needed, and the programme ran very smoothly with no big problems.

Test results were recorded and sent off to Australia and the car went into low-volume production there.

This was another programme which demonstrated the ability of MG Design and Development to adapt to almost any type of build and testing when required.

P76 Australian BMC saloon development from a special engineering programme.

MGB V8

In May 1971 Syd Enever retired from MG Design and Roy Brocklehurst became Chief Engineer, responsible for the current production of MGB and Midgets. One of his first jobs was to design the installation of the Rover V8 engine for production in the MGB.

Design Office was to look at the Costello version already on the market, which firm was converting standard MGBs and modifying them to accept the Rover V8 saloon engine. Assessment of the Costello revealed several points were not directly acceptable to MG Chassis Design. The steering column had a welded joint in it which was felt to not be of approved quality for production, so a new flexible joint and location were installed. Minor improvements were made to the exhaust system and joints, and the carburettors and bonnet bulge area changed. Alec Hounslow proposed a new inlet manifold layout which Barrie Jackson designed in detail, using a pair of SU HS6 carburettors, obviating the need for a change to bonnet shape. With the forward radiator position of later MGBs and MGCs a larger capacity cooling with twin fans was possible, and the design was confirmed.

On American emission versions of the engines with exhaust port air injection pump and pipes, extra crash testing at 30mph was carried out. As the V8 was aluminium alloy, it was not much different in weight to the standard 'B' series – maybe 40lb lighter – so no big problems were encountered. The exhaust system – from twin cylinder banks merging into one for the silencer – had to be carefully aligned so that, in rearward motion in a crash, the fuel tank was not damaged.

With new engines available from Rover, and new alloy valve rocker boxes, with the MG badge moulded on the top of the cover, road testing started. Initial standing start tests soon revealed that the version of the MGB gearbox used failed in bottom gear due to the much higher torque available from the V8 engine, the largest unit used in an MG, ever. A stronger, 16-toothed gear replaced the 17-toothed version, and this was okay.

A new road wheel had been considered by Enever when offered by Dunlop, which was already available on the Triumph Stag. This he approved with the proviso that the sharp corners on the cooling vent apertures be smoothed off. This composite steel rim, riveted and glued to the alloy centre, was to be tested to MG standards at Dunlop. The report came back that the test was stopped as the wheel was as strong as the test machine, achieving 1,000,000 reversals.

New tyres of 175xHR14 were being specially made for the model by Dunlop, and were supplied for road test, so Alec Hounslow and Tom Haig did many miles at high speed, and in handling areas. Comments from them and Dunlop test drivers also involved were that the cars appeared to wander off a straight line, and at speed. No fault could be found in the steering mechanisms so the tyres were investigated. Dunlop Production found that control in assembly of the built-in steel belt was not tight enough, allowing loads to the tyre sidewalls to vary, causing sideloading effects. Assembly control was improved, and the tyre approved for the V8.

Rover produced at least eight American specification engines, and six production cars were built for Sales to send to the USA for market approval. We put one on the test bed for horsepower rating, and held a spare. With 30mph crash testing passed okay, the car was cleared for USA distributors to proceed, but as

August 1973 MGB GT V8 demonstrator press release car.

This development V8, which was raced by Bob Neville, was bought and modified by Malcolm Beer.

Rover was withdrawing from the States, the V8 was then cancelled.

A special production line for the V8 had been running in A Block, but the volume of cars produced was decided by the quantity of available engines from Rover.

While all this had been going on, in August 1973 Roy B, my Chief Engineer, said to me: "Get in my car, we're going to Longbridge." Once on the road, he said: "You, Don, are now Chief Engineer of MG. I have been transferred as Chief Vehicle Engineer Austin Rover also covering MG but moving to Longbridge." So, my first job was to launch the V8 into production.

The next decision I made was to change all of our designs to meet American Safety Regulations for more severe emissions controls, crash testing, and driver safety.

The V8 acquired rubber bumpers in parallel with the MGB, a safety steering column, and very nearly airbags, which, luckily, were suspended and never featured on any production MG.

V8 production finally closed because of senior management's decision to stop the supply of engines from Rover – the low volume supplied to MG did not justify continuation.

ADO 21

Future plans for an MGB replacement from the 'powers-that-be'

In 1969, the directors, via our new ex-Triumph Chief Engineer, Harry Webster, initiated a new programme to design a mid-engine MG, in line with the development of Grand Prix racing cars at the time. MG immediately produced a scheme for a modified GT body using the available E series four-cylinder engine with a completely new rear suspension. This was a Mitchell version using a rear de Dion axle tube with control links and sprung shock absorbers. The centre of the de Dion tube was a ball joint that provided thrust to a socket on the existing MGB heelboard, and centre tunnel of the chassis floor: an unusual method of transmitting the drive.

I was provided with a design facility in Longbridge, and, using this system, drew up a new chassis package on which a new coupé body shape was based. This was intended to replace the MGB, with styling done by Harris Mann in Longbridge Styling. The initial design proposed was very wedge-shaped, as a continuation of various ideas carried forward from the Ambassador model, and earlier in the 'Zanda project' by Harris Mann.

During the final period when Enever was in charge, he had designs drawn up for a new front suspension with tall shock absorber spring wheel control arms. This system I incorporated into the ADO 21 new chassis design on a drawing board layout to secure approval for a prototype. At the same time, Triumph Design, under John Lloyd and Derek Peck, was working on a new project called Lynx, plus another alternative.

Some development mileage was done on our MGB GT modified version, which was beginning to produce

MGB GT with transverse 'E Series' 2-litre sports engine in the rear.

GT rear suspension de Dion tube rear axle, springs and shock absorbers. Ball joint centre bracket connection.

results with an acceptable ride, using the Maxi Sports 2-litre E series engine.

This programme – and eventually the Triumph one – was first suspended and then cancelled as review of the BMC-Austin Rover Company changes began. MG did no further work ,and the prototype was shelved and finally scrapped.

My personal opinion was that, although the Harris Mann design was pushing styling forward, it was not in the direction I would have liked it to go. The engineering part of the exercise was good experience, however, and might well have helped if we were allowed to go our

AD021 mid-engine styled for MG by Harris Mann at Longbridge Styling.

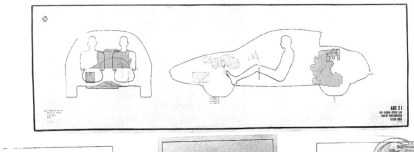

Alternative AD021 styles.

Pressed Steel, Oxford, styled package by Jim Oates on AD021, coded 'Apollo.'

own route. Certainly, control of the power unit via pedals at the front to a rear-mounted power unit necessitated components such as long throttle cables, or electrical systems to be designed and developed. Also crash testing with quite a different weight distribution introduced completely new structural problems.

All of these ideas had to be shelved as we were directed onto the Austin- Rover-Triumph link programme with Honda, and europeanising of the Ballade was officially begun.

O series

During the early 1970s, compliance with the increasingly severe American and Canadian emissions standards reduced the MGB's and Midget's performance. Since American/Canadian sales were such a big proportion of our market, we had to comply but, obviously, new and more suitable power units were needed. Design work at Longbridge involved development of new engines, and the O series at 1.7- and 2.0-litres, and the S series at 1.1- to 1.4-litres were to be available in transverse or inline forms.

One of the first prototype engines, in 2-litre form and fitted with a standard MGB gearbox, came to MG Development to be installed in a GT body. This needed new engine mountings, exhaust system, and harness connections, but not much else, and went straight onto road test, durability, fuel consumption and noise testing. This first unit was fitted with SU carburettors and new air cleaners with very few problems.

However, we did find that the cambelt covers – which were metal pressings – vibrated to a point that an engine fault was suspected, but, when stripped, no fault was found. One day the car came in from a development run and the driver reported something like a detonation ring and vibration. On looking at the engine with the cambelt cover removed, I said to Pat Cox, the foreman, "Is the cambelt supposed to be that narrow?" It should obviously have been about an inch wide, but had a feathery edge and was only ¼ in wide.

The car ran okay, and valve timing was apparently unaffected, but the clue was that on the crankshaft pulley was a formed metal disc with a slot in it, to allow the timing marker to be seen. Experimental demonstrated the disc vibrated just enough to touch the edge of the cambelt, and continually machine off a bit; the frequency was audible down the crankshaft as well. A small pressing redesign at Longbridge was done and all was well.

In 1978 we were authorised to make prototypes of the MGB with a Stromberg carburettor setup, similar to the one on the existing B series engine but with an O series engine management system. Our Design Directors were by now Triumph-based at Canley, and were looking at a Chrysler 'lean-burn' system developed in the USA, which could be purchased and adapted for our cars. This involved fitting a PCB (electronic control circuit board), and a group of prototypes were ordered. No money was allocated at this point for any body styling or similar improvements – badly needed as the B was now 15 years old. Development by the emissions laboratory and on the cars was not satisfactory, and my Director, John Lloyd, told me to start work on a new system.

This was to be a Lucas Jetronic fuel injection system involving a quite new underbonnet layout and fuel supply. Engines were built fairly quickly by Longbridge Development under John Barnett, involving new inlet manifolds and exhausts. Emission testing prospects were good with a much improved horsepower rating. Lucas, at Great King St, had developed an electronic control box for the Jaguar V12 for America, so we negotiated four cylinders' worth of flat black box to fit into a protected stable mounting area on the MGB. Consequently, the last few authentic O series prototypes have a rectangular hole in the side footwell panel, behind the trim pad where the harness would have run out into the front wing cavity behind the splash plate.

In order to increase fuel supply capacity a new electric pump system was proposed for the larger engine.

One system tested was an American GM submerged pump inside the existing fuel tank! This worked well. An alternative was a Facet pump: in effect, a pulsating coil box which gave very high performance when mounted in place of the SU pump. Either would have done, with probably cost and service dictating the Facet. Two early cars were sent out to Cosenza in southern Italy in parallel with some Sherpa vans using similar engines for high-speed durability running – the Sherpa was using the MGB overdrive, too.

The test programme had expanded to allow bodies to be proved with the pressing changes done at Pressed Steel at Swindon to come through on the line. This explains why cars have GHN5 production numbers allocated by MG, although B series engines were never fitted, and bodies were built to B standard and then manually pushed or towed to development.

A group of these cars were built to USA standard for emission and crash testing to obtain compliance data for introduction to the market as a new model. There were to be no external body styling changes or improvements other than a side stripe identification of a new model! Two cars were allocated to go with a team to America for environmental hot climate test and high altitude emissions and performance assessment.

In Sept '75 we booked to fly out to Dallas from Gatwick with two cars numbered L4 and L6 on the programme. L4 was UJO 786T and L6 was RUD 223T, both of them MGB Tourers in full American spec. They went out to run on the high-speed circuit, and did the emissions and cooling testing in or around New Orleans. This was where Graham Gardiner, from BL Leonia, came down to meet them and confirm the results. MG Development staff – who Basil remembers being involved in this – were Don Sollis, from the Cowley office, Barry Trewin, Steve Grey, and Basil Smith himself. They also flew on to Denver for emission testing at altitude, and monitoring of the engine management system.

Several O series engines were fitted to MGBs by Abingdon. At least six MGBs in fully federalized emissions control condition went to America, and did some running at Galveston using the high-speed circuit for emission testing, water temperature, and all the other things needed to pass the American federal tests. I have a letter on file from Graham Gardiner to say that this was the best MG ever for cooling, and very successful with the new big radiator in the forward position.

Two or three cars were fitted with the European twin carburetter engine as opposed to the fuel injected American units, and my car is one of these. The engine was taken out and went back to Triumph when the factory closed, and my car was converted to the V8 that it is today.

One further GT was built with a Garret turbocharged system in it, which we ran very successfully for some time. It was producing something like 160bhp: a very quick motor car. The problem was that we did not have the money or time to get a proper exhaust manifold made, and therefore had to use a fabricated one. This suffered from continual cracking due to the high temperatures experienced in a turbocharged engine. As far as I remember, the programme called for something like 24 cars in the programme, allowing for crash testing as well, but bear in mind, of course, that the O series fuel injected system which we were using – the Lucas Bosch 'Jetronic' – was superseding something we had worked on earlier: the Triumph-based idea of the Chrysler lean-burn system on the engine with a very large PC board under the bonnet as an engine management system.

A lot of these cars were built as ADO number cars, whereas the later ones which had the full modifications to the wheelarches, forward radiator position, and engine mountings were built down the line in Swindon, with modifications to test out pressing feasibility and all the rest of it, so that the bodyshell was ready to run in production. My car is one of these.

The decision to close MG meant the end of the programme.

We had one special job left to do which was to install an engine in an Ambassador for Ray Bates, Director at Longbridge Design, as a one-off. This was fitted in a car provided to Development, and supplied in running – but completely untested or developed – form.

We had no further details of this programme and did not see the car again. The turbocharged engine went to Longbridge Engines, and was not heard of again.

My feeling was that the MGB might just have run on in production for maybe a couple of years with some panel face-lifts, because of American support. A completely new-style body, and chassis and suspension design as programmed, was needed.

I gather that the proposal to use our developed O series unit in the Triumph TR7 was considered, but did not get American support.

Finally, Triumph Sports Cars also closed, ending a long British involvement in the American market.

The beginning of the end

Aston Martin takeover & Honda involvement

Toward the end of 1979 we were working steadily on final design and development of installation in the MGB of the O series engine. Mentions were appearing in the press, and rumours filtered through from company departments in the Midlands. We were not kept informed, and it was only through the works and MG Car Club that any of my staff were able to be involved in the 'Save MG' campaign. I was informally directed to keep clear until official policy was decided, and instructions issued. My brief was to supply details of the O programme to Roy Brocklehurst and Longbridge Director Alan Edis for their status reports and discussions with Aston Martin.

I was told that a meeting with Aston Martin directors was being arranged, and that Design was required to confirm MG compliance levels with all USA Federal regulations. All Design and Development sections duly provided this with an estimate of hours and work needed to sign off the programme at an agreed takeover date to be decided.

I went with John Symons, our Cowley Director, to the Randolf Hotel in Oxford to meet Alan Curtis, Financial Director of Aston Martin, to examine feasibility and hand over our initial documents and requests. Aston Martin had requested a car from MG as part of the negotiations, so that a styling exercise could be done for modified bumpers, but this was refused. No external body changes had been involved or approved for the 'B' O series; the most we had done was to add a special side-stripe running from front to rear bumpers.

Olson Laboratories was approached to carry out an add-on modification for carburation and exhaust systems to ensure the MGB in 'B' series format was compliant for the next (1981) model year. This would allow the necessary changes over time for build and supply of O series engines to production.

A revision of the product plan was also needed for the developing Austin-Morris Honda programme, to which my team was committed. My job was to coordinate the engineering programme, and ensure that the Honda – now codenamed Bounty – was ready for UK production: the body built in the UK and engine supplied from Suzuka in Japan. Prototypes were to be high-speed and durability tested in Germany. The basic MGB programme was to continue until Vehicle Engineering assessed the proposed new marketing conditions being negotiated between Austin Morris and Aston Martin.

In the event, no agreement was reached, and a statement was issued confirming that MG would cease production in October 1980.

Design and Development were transferred to offices in Cowley Body Plant and Morris Experimental next door, where the Honda project was to run. We acquired an enormous fax machine directly linked to Japan for information and drawing transfer. Having made sure all of my Development staff had jobs to move on to in Design or Service where possible, I carried on, making several visits to Honda Design in Japan. The Bounty programme used the basic Ballade model with cosmetic changes. This programme included testing to European standards for crash tests and vehicle compliance, and was completed and signed off.

I was offered a move to Coventry, but as I didn't wish to leave the Abingdon area, I chose early retirement

End of the MGB line – staff group for the visit of John Thornley and Syd Enever. Production now ended.

instead. I had, at every opportunity, been going back to Abingdon to oversee the final closure of the factory, until my old colleague, Doug Gardner, had to authorise shutting of the gates.

In parallel with these changes we had been allocated development workshop space in the old Morris factory next door to the Pressed Steel Body Plant. The Bounty (codename for the Triumph Acclaim) road test programme ran from there, and was closed as soon as all testing was completed. Some of the staff and mechanics were found jobs in Unipart, also at Cowley, and some eventually took redundancy. I left, having negotiated permission to take away as many records as I could: the instructions from above being to "put it all in the skip," so many of the old documents were lost. All drawings and drafts were saved by being sent to Gaydon stores (British Motor Heritage Museum).

But this was not the end of the MGB's story. David Bishop (Managing Director of British Motor Heritage) noted the interest in the replacement panel pressings

The best use of an MGB: with grandchildren at Harwell Feast in my V8, May 2005.

in his workshop setup in Faringdon, where major parts were being manufactured using original press tools. From this base, the car was resurrected at Cowley in the form of the RV8 on a new production line. This model contained the latest form of the Rover V8 fuel injected engine, and updated suspension. In fact, just what we at MG, Abingdon had hoped to produce one day. The car was a great success in Japan.

I still run an MG, my own V8 tourer, to rallies and events, and have acquired a 'grandchild support team' with which to attend the car parades at the local Harwell Feast.

Bibliography

Maintaining the Breed: the saga of MG racing cars by John W Thornley Motor Racing Publications Ltd

The Story of the MG Sports Car by F Wilson McComb Osprey Publishing Ltd ISBN: 0850453100

BMC/BL Competitions Department: 25 Years in Motorsport: The Cars, the People, the Events by Bill Price Haynes Publishing ISBN: 0854296778

The Magic of the Marque by Mike Allison The Pen & Ink Book Company Ltd ISBN: 0901564-826

Original MGB: with MGC and MGB GT V8 by Anders Ditlev Clausager Bay View Books Ltd ISBN: 1870979486

MGB The Illustrated History by Jonathan Wood & Lionel Burrell Haynes Publishing ISBN: 0854295992

MGB The Untold Story by David Knowles Windrow & Green Ltd ISBN: 1859150519

MG's Abingdon Factory – Brian J Moylan Veloce Publishing Ltd ISBN: 9781845841140

Also from Veloce –

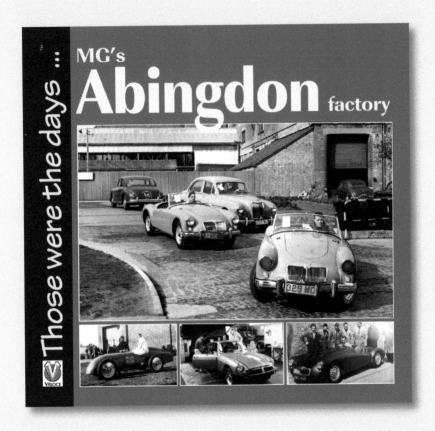

Those were the days ...™

MG's Abingdon factory

ISBN: 978-1-787111-15-8
Paperback • 19x20.5cm • 96 pages • 164 colour and b&w pictures

The MG, from being a Morris car modified in the corner of a backstreet workshop, evolved into a sports car in its own right. The 164 pictures in this book – many never seen before – chronicle every aspect of the MG Abingdon factory from its opening amidst great euphoria in 1930 to its closing amidst great recrimination in 1980.

For more info on Veloce titles, visit our website at www.veloce.co.uk • email: info@veloce.co.uk • Tel: +44(0)1305 260068

Also from Veloce –

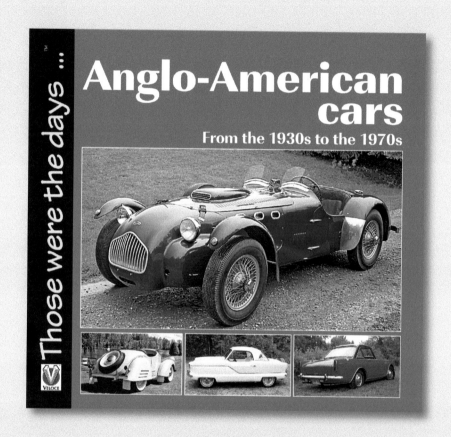

ISBN: 978-1-845842-33-8
Paperback • 19x20.5cm • 96 pages • 103 colour and b&w pictures

Covers British cars powered by American engines and American cars fitted with British power plants, all built from the 1930s to the 1970s. The first book dedicated solely to these unique hybrids bearing both American and British engineering, made for those who lust to drive something different.

For more info on Veloce titles, visit our website at www.veloce.co.uk • email: info@veloce.co.uk • Tel: +44(0)1305 260068

Also from Veloce –

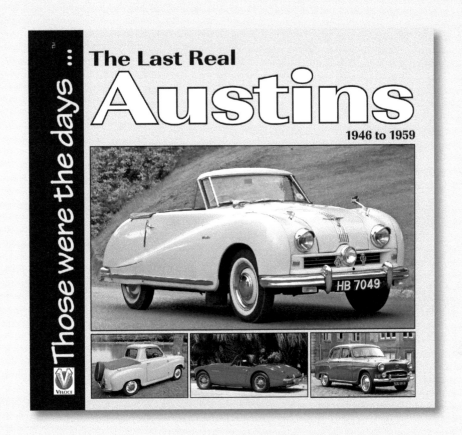

Those were the days ...™

The Last Real
Austins
1946 to 1959

VELOCE

ISBN: 978-1-787111-12-7
Paperback • 19x20.5cm • 96 pages • 89 colour and b&w pictures

This book examines how Austin bounced back after WWII, and how, despite the severe materials shortage, it managed to develop the largest range of vehicles produced by any automaker in postwar Britain. Illustrated with 100 pictures, many of them rare archive photographs, depicting the weird and wonderful – and the downright imaginative.

For more info on Veloce titles, visit our website at www.veloce.co.uk • email: info@veloce.co.uk • Tel: +44(0)1305 260068

Also from Veloce –

ISBN: 978-1-787110-54-0
Paperback • 19.5x13.9cm • 64 pages • 114 colour and b&w pictures

A small investment in this book could save you a fortune ... With the aid of this book's step-by-step expert guidance, you'll discover all you need to know about the car you want to buy. Unique point system will help you to place the car's value in relation to condition. This is an important investment – don't buy a car without this book's help.

For more info on Veloce titles, visit our website at www.veloce.co.uk • email: info@veloce.co.uk • Tel: +44(0)1305 260068

Index